GRINDHOUSE PU
Vol. 1, Issue 5

Contents

HEADITORIAL:	2
GONE BUT NEVER FORGOTTEN	4
REMEMBERING JOHN FASANO	6
REMEMBERING OX BAKER	11
12 HOURS ON "THE DEUCE" REVISITED	14
THE BLAXPLOITATION FILMS	20
TRUCK TURNER	27
42P's TOP TWENTY BLAXPLOITATION FILMS	29
THE ENSEMBLE CAST: A GRINDHOUSE STAPLE	30
RED SUN:	34
SCOTT WILSON'S FIVE DECADES IN FILM	36
AWKWARD THANKSGIVING	39
MAKING POLLEN	41
THE MIDNIGHT MOVIE	44
NOTHING TO SEE HERE!	47
THE GIRLS OF *42ND STREET* & *FORCED ENTRY* (1973)	49
LUIGI COZZI'S STAR CRASH	53
CRIMINALLY INSANE	58
RAW FORCE	61
WITHOUT WARNING	64
INTERVIEW WITH SCOTT MAYER	66
TONY ANTHONY: THE STRANGER	72
REVIEWS	74
SO SAYETH: BUBBA THE REDNECK WEREWOLF	76
THE PRINCE OF DARKNESS: KEVIN SULLIVAN	80
A GUIDE TO THE DEATHMATCH	83
CUMMING SOON	86
CHESTY MORGAN: AN IMPERFECT PAIR	90
TURNING BACK THE HANDS OF SLIME	95
DESIRE FOR MEN	96

Publisher and Editor-in-Chief: Pete Chiarella. Editor-in-General: Mike Watt.
Layout: Amy Lynn Best
Contributors: Bill Adcock, Dr. Rhonda Baughman, Josh Hadley, Cory Udler

© 2014 by 42nd Street Pete Chiarella.
No part of this publication can be duplicated in any way without express permission of the publisher. Except for the pictures. The pictures we already stole. Knock yourself out.

HEADITORIAL:
THE DEATH OF FILM, THE WHORING OUT OF OUR FILMS, AND THE CON IS OVER

First, to the people who took time to post some positive things about our last issue, we thank you. I also thank the people who contributed to it, especially Gary Kent, Carter Stevens, and Cory Udler, who scored that great Ted V. Mikels interview. All of the writers love what they do and that love bleeds all over these pages. Again, special thanks to our editor, Mike Watt, who was going through some really horrible stuff last year, but took the time to have *GP # 4* ready for Cinema Wasteland.

Sadly, actual film is dead. The studios, in their infinite corporate wisdom, have forced theaters to go with digital projection. Check out the great documentary, *Out of Print*, directed by Julia Marchese. A former New Beverly employee who really knows her stuff and put this great film together. Studios are transferring their film libraries to digital. If that isn't bad enough, I was told that film prints were dumped into the Atlantic Ocean to dispose of them. Our corporate cheapskates don't want to pay to store film prints. Nor do they want to sell them, because perish the thought of someone owning an actual film.

Julia Marchese was on my radio show and explained that digital media is already showing signs of corruption. Film, be it 8mm. 16mm, or 35mm has held up since the turn of the century. Sure, there are problems with film, color fading, vinegar syndrome, breakage, splices, etc. But you can fix it. Some of these films have lasted 100 years; can you say the same for video tape, laser discs, DVDs, or Blu-Rays? No, you can't. Video tape has a 20 to 30 year shelf life, plus it can get moldy if stored in a basement or attic. Laser discs, the supposed wet dream for film collectors, were abandoned for the DVD. Just as well as the discs got 'laser rot' as glue was used to put discs together. Glue, being a solvent, would eat its way through one side of the disc, pixelating the picture. Now I'm hearing about problems with Blu-Rays.

I don't go to theaters anymore as I'm not paying to sit and watch a DVD. For the steep admission price, I'll buy it when it comes out, then trade it in to Half Price Books for probably .50 cents, as DVDs seem to have little resale value unless they are completely out of print. Yeah, *Doom Asylum, Emmanuelle and the Last Cannibals, Eaten Alive*, and others are over $100 each on Amazon. DVDs have become disposable. Piles of them at flea markets for $1 each. Companies have cheapened our movies by putting 3 to 4 films on a DVD. Even worse, some are showing up in $1 Stores. Even the mighty Blu-Ray is being blown out in some locations for $5 and under. Great for the consumer, but the discount whoring them out by studios just pisses me off. When you grow up watching these films, it hurts to see them treated like bargain basement junk.

Right now there are so many horror conventions that they are all pretty much shitty, mirror images of each other. I have been involved in these things since 1990 when Horrorthon came into being. The name was changed to Chiller Theater. That show was the ultimate shopping experience for fans. 25 years later, there is a glut of really crappy conventions run by con artists, felons, grifters, and the like. They have the same tired-out guests, they give you very little for the price of admission, and they battle on the internet, some staying on Facebook during the show to *delete* negative comments made about their show. If they put half the effort into their shows instead that they do posting on FB, maybe fans wouldn't have to post negative comments. Even worse is when their featured "guest" cancels out a week before the show, which seems to be the norm for some cons. Just look at Geekfest in Dayton, Ohio, last year. Every headliner canceled.

The latest bitching was about something called Walker Stalker, a convention geared to fans of the show *The Walking Dead*. People connected with other cons were pitching a bitch about the high prices, guest autographs, etc. *The Walking Dead* is this generation's *Star Trek*. These are not fuckin' horror fans; they are people unbothered by the high ticket price because this is an event. With very few exceptions, the cast of *The Walking Dead* were not in any horror films. So comparing that con to Chiller, Horrorhound, DOTD, Monster Mania, etc., is like comparing apples to turnips: two completely different things. But a bitch was pitched by some followers of other certain conventions over the high tickets. Hey, if you fuckers thought of it first, you'd be doing it.

Problem as I see it is that the same guests appear at just about every show. Another problem: huge internet balls. I got my profile deleted from Facebook because I spoke out against certain people bullying newcomers to the scene. Now I'm not even talking about conventions on FB or on my radio show. Someone said, 'does that go for Cinema Wasteland, too?' No, because CW isn't a convention. It's a show where you get over 60 hours of entertaining programming, be it films, panels, indie screenings, etc. It isn't about the guests, it's about the films. And CW does have great guests, not the flavor of the day. You want Kane Hodder, Tony Todd, Robert Englund, Roddy Piper, Bill Mosely, etc.? Cool, you can find them everywhere except Wasteland. And I'm not knocking these guys, but face facts, a lot of them have become professional convention guests. Sadly I see the end coming for these cons as they are the same broken record.

It will be exactly one year since Mike Vraney and Al Goldstein left us. It's been a couple of years since we lost our friend Andy Copp. We started *GP* as a tribute to Andy. I honestly never thought it would go more than that issue. We are thankful that you, the reader, dig what we do. It isn't easy putting this together. Other than Amazon, we have no distribution, nor do I take paid ads. I keep it real. *GP* gives people the opportunity to write. If anyone reading this would like to contribute something, cool, show me what you got. Email me at fortydeuce@hotmail.com. Got a film or genre you'd like to see us cover? Cool, let us know.

People have asked if I'm doing a follow up to my *Gunfighters of the Drunken Master*. Yeah, I'm working on it, but you can't rush something like this. The book got a lot of positive reviews, so I want to make the 2nd one just as good or better. The Blindman, Nydia, Dog, Leo, Lee, and The Shotgun Girls are back. Without giving too much away, think *The Magnificent Seven* on crack. Working title is *Unhappy Hour*. So until next issue, stay sick.—XXXX, 42nd Street Pete

GONE BUT NEVER FORGOTTEN

I decided to create this feature for GP to honor the people who did great work in film. Be it Grindhouse or mainstream, these performers entertained us in the most pivotal era of film making the world has ever known, 1962 to 1987.

Strother Martin (1919-1980) from Kokomo, IN. Served in the navy during WWII. His turn as the warden in *Cool Hand Luke* made him one of the busiest character actors around. He dabbled in all kinds of films: *Sssss, Hannie Calder, Brotherhood of Satan, The Wild Bunch* (he was a Peckinpah regular), *Cheech & Chong's Up in Smoke*, and many others. He was at the peak of his career when he passed away from a heart attack in 1980

Vonetta McGee (1945-2010) from San Francisco, CA. In the seldom seem *The Great Silence*, she had what was the first interracial love scene with Jean-Louis Trintignant. Her role in *Blacula* gave her career a huge boost. She was in *Hammer, Detroit 9000, The Eiger Sanction, Brothers, Repo Man*, and others. She died from cardiac arrest in 2010.

R.G. Armstrong (1917-2012) from Birmingham, AL. The over-six-foot-tall actor never lacked for work. He did a lot of TV westerns where he met Sam Peckinpah and became one of his stock players in films like *Major Dundee* and *Pat Garrett and Billy the Kid*. He did everything from horror to comedy. *The Car, Beast Within, Race with the Devil, Steel, Dick Tracy, Payback* and others. He died of natural causes at age 95.

John Mitchum (1919-2001) was the younger, by two years, brother of Robert Mitchum. He worked with Eastwood (first three *Dirty Harry* films, *The Outlaw Josey Wales*) Bronson (*Telefon, Breakheart Pass*) Did a lot of Television work and films like *Bigfoot, Bandolero, Chandler, The Bloody Trail*, and others. He was 82.

George "Buck" Flower (1937-2004) was in an incredible group of films ranging from low budget porn to A-pictures. He worked for Harry Novak, Don Edmunds, John Carpenter, Nick Phillips, and many more. He used several other names like "C.L. LeFleur", "Sherman Backus" and "Lloyd Mathews". Whether it was 5 seconds or 15 minutes in a film, George made an impact with over 150 film credits, including *They Live* and *Sorority Babes in the Slimeball Bowl-O-Rama*. He died at age 66 of cancer.

Bryon Sanders (1925-2001) from Charlotte, NC, was in 1964's *The Flesh Eaters* and *Trick, Baby* in 1972. He did a lot of TV and was the model for the Salvatore Dali painting, *Crucifixion*, which now hangs in the Metropolitan Museum of Art. He was 76.

Kent Taylor (1907-1987) from Nashua, IA, was a popular B actor in the '30s and '40s, appearing in A-pictures as a second lead. He was in over 100 films, played *Boston Blackie* on TV and did a lot of appearances on TV westerns. Toward the end of his career, he was in *The Crawling Hand, Phantom from 10,000 Leagues, Brides of Blood, Satan's Sadists, Girls for Rent* and *Hell's Bloody Devils*. He died in 1987 from complications from heart surgery.

Neville Brand (1920-1992) was one of the most highly-decorated servicemen coming out of WWII. He played Al Capone 3 times, in *The George Raft Story*, *The Scarface Mob* and TV's *The Untouchables*. He was Reese Bennett in the TV series *Laredo*. He was in *Birdman of Alcatraz*, *Tora, Tora, Tora*, *Cahill US Marshall*, and other "A" pictures. Toward the end of his career he appeared in several horror films, *The Psychic Killer*, *Eaten Alive*, and *Without Warning*. Tragically his last film was the abysmal *Evils of the Night*.

Al Mulock (1926-1968) was from Canada. He studied acting under Lee Strasburg in NYC, then moved to Great Britain, where he and David DeKeyser opened The London Studio where they taught method acting to British actors. He was very involved in British film and television. He was in two *Tarzan* movies: *Tarzan's Greatest Adventure* (1959) and *Tarzan the Magnificent* (1960), both with Gordon Scott. He did a lot of Spaghetti Westerns. He was the one armed bounty hunter in *The Good, the Bad, and The Ugly*, the beggar in *The Hellbenders*, co-starred with Lee Van Cleef in *Day of Anger*, and was one of the killers waiting for Charles Bronson in *Once Upon a Time in the West*. He committed suicide on that film by jumping out the window of his hotel while in costume. Writer Mickey Knox claimed he was a drug addict and may have killed himself because he couldn't get drugs on location in Spain.

John Davis Chandler (1935-2010) Specialized in playing oily, psychotic heavies. He started out as the lead in 1961's *Mad Dog Coll* and appeared in *The Young Savages* the same year. He did a lot of TV work, then went to work for Sam Peckinpah in *Ride the High Country* (1962) as one of the Hammond Brothers with LQ Jones, Warren Oates, and James Drury. He stayed with Sam for *Major Dundee* and *Pat Garrett and Billy the Kid*. He was a great heavy in westerns like *Barquero*, *Good Guys and Bad Guys*, and *The Outlaw Josey Wales*. He worked for Florida based Bill Grefe in *The Hooked Generation* and *Mako: Jaws of Death*. He did a lot more TV work in the '80s and appeared in *Sword and the Sorcerer*, *Crash and Burn*, *Carnosaur 2*, and *Phantasm 3*.

REMEMBERING JOHN FASANO
By Cory Udler

On July 19th we lost John Fasano. If you're unfamiliar with John he is the man behind '80s gems such as *Rock N Roll Nightmare*, *The Jitters*, and *Black Roses*. John was also a prolific writer with *Another 48 Hours* and *The Legend of Butch and Sundance* to his credit. John was also a recipient of the U.S. Army's Commander's Award for Public Service for his writing and directing of Army Strong-Technology of the 21st Century. John was a renaissance man and one of the nicest guys I've ever had the pleasure of getting to know. Granted, I never had the chance to shake John's hand, but we had a great correspondence and he was a guest on my old Astro Radio Z online radio show. In the last year Derrick (*Swamphead, Hole in the Wall*) Carey and I worked a bit with John to get the wheels moving on a *Black Roses 2*. That idea, while stuck due to monetary issues, still lives. We owe it to John to do it now. Or at least try.

My first exposure to John was through *Black Roses*. Children of the VHS boom remember that 3D slipcase. It was gorgeous. So perfect. And the movie remains in my top 5 of all time to this day. Heavy metal, demons, hot chicks. What's not to love? Over the years I discovered some of his other work in directing, art, and writing. John was an amazing artist with a pen and did a lot of work for *G-Fan Magazine*.

My friendship with John also led me to getting to know Sal Viviano and Frank Dietz, stars of several of John's films including *Black Roses*. I reached out to them shortly after John's passing to see if they would be willing to share some of their memories and pay tribute to him.

If you are unfamiliar with John's work I can only hope that you'll seek out his art after reading this. We love you, John. We'll all miss you. We'll never forget you and we'll continue to celebrate your legacy and carry on in your shadow.

Frank Dietz is best known to horror fans as "Johnny" in *Black Roses* and "Roger Eburt" in *Rock N Roll Nightmare*. But Frank has one of the most impressive resumes in all of cinema to his credit including his work as an animator on many Disney movies including *Mulan* and *Hercules*. A writer, producer, director, and cinematographer, Frank is a busy dude and we were honored that he took the time out to spend a few minutes with us here at *Grindhouse Purgatory* to talk about the late, great John Fasano.

Frank Dietz: *John Fasano and I met when we were still in elementary school. We grew up in the same town on the north shore of Long Island. We discovered that we shared a love of monsters and all things fantastic. We also shared an innate artistic ability, so we spent countless hours drawing and painting our favorite Ray Harryhausen characters, Universal Monsters and talking apes. We'd spend our summers shooting Super 8mm mini-movies starring our Aurora plastic Godzilla models. We didn't know it, but we were cultivating the seeds of what would eventually become our careers in the film industry.*

*Many years later, John called me out of the blue to tell me that a horror movie he wrote was being made. It was called **Zombie Nightmare** and John suggested that I audition for one of the lead roles. I got that part, and so began a crazy rollercoaster ride into the world of low budget horror films.*

We made four feature films between 1985 and 1989, all shot in Canada, and all have achieved cult notoriety over the years. John's vision was audacious, outlandish, and always just plain fun. When the films were first released, a lot of people didn't understand that, following John's lead, we knew exactly what we were making.

*The third film of the group was **Black Roses**, the metal-rock-band-from-Hell creature fest. John referred to me as his "Ward Bond", which is a reference that only fans of old John Wayne westerns could understand. It meant that I was his go-to actor, the one he could count on to play any role he assigned me. This time that role would be "Johnny Pratt", a seventeen-year-old angst ridden and lovesick student who falls prey to the siren's call of Damian and his Black Roses. I was twenty-eight at the time, so playing ten years younger required both a mental and physical transformation, which John helped me prepare for. The role called for a buck-naked sex scene, as my character is seduced by one of Damian's female minions. John requested that I shave off all of my chest hair, to further the illusion that I was a high school student. He was right. It worked aesthetically, but also helped me get into my character's head.*

We shot the majority of the film in a town outside of Toronto called Hamilton. John recruited a crowd of actual high school students to fill the classroom seats and hallways of the school we were shooting in. These kids were great, and I think they were really excited to be a part of a real movie. But not all of the town's denizens were so pleased with our invasion of their turf. One night, shooting on a quiet residential street, a disgruntled neighbor threatened to call the cops on us. We were later told that the man had a shotgun ready to unload on us if we stepped even one foot onto his property. On another night shoot, we had the entire main drag of the town closed to shoot some important scenes of the village turning violent under Damian's control. Karen Planden ("Julie") and I were shooting a dialogue scene when suddenly we heard a commotion nearby. It was one in the morning and the local bar had just released their intoxicated patrons, many of which were unhappy about our presence. They came looking for a fight and there were some very tense moments before the police showed up to quiet the riot. Personally, I think John could have taken them all on himself, but that would have interfered with the always important matter at hand-getting the shot!

*I have so many stories of making those films with John that I could fill an entire book with them. And I just might. Thanks to John, I went on to become a screenwriter, a Disney Animator, a producer, and director. Recently I produced and directed an award-winning documentary called **Beast Wishes**, and am currently preparing to shoot a feature called **American Vampires**. All of these accomplishments can be directly, or indirectly, traced back to my work and friendship with John Fasano. His talent, his influence, and his humor will be with me always.*

In addition to Frank Dietz, I reached out to another of John's "go-to" actors, Sal Viviano, who we all know as Damian in *Black Roses*. Sal also portrayed "Michael" in John's film *The Jitters*. Sal sat down and shared his thoughts on John.

John Fasano and Sal Viviano – BLACK ROSES Production Still

Sal Viviano: *I first met John Fasano when I auditioned for* **Black Roses**. *I remember taking the train out to Bronxville, New York to be put on tape at his home. Kind of an unusual situation, but my agent and I both thought that the role of Damian, as described on the casting notice, seemed like a good fit. John was articulate, charismatic, and informal in a very generous way with information about his vision for the film and the role. He and his wife, Cindy Sorrell, who had written the script, spent a great deal of time with me that day, and also had me read for the role of the teacher, Matt Moorehouse, before I left. The connection, for me, was immediate. I knew I wanted to know these good folks, and hoped to get the opportunity to participate in their vision.*

Looking back at the audition footage that is included on the **BR** *DVD, with the choice and witty commentary by John and Cindy throughout, I have to admit I laughed out loud seeing myself in that baby blue jacket for one thing. Wow! But, it also made me appreciate all the more John's vision at being able to see whatever it is directors see that convinces them that someone is right to tell their story. Through the ensuing months of pre-production, including casting sessions with the make-up effects artists of my head, eyes, and various other body parts (ahem) for the sculpted appliances that I would eventually wear in the film, while turning in to the several stages of the Damian monster, John and I hit it off great. I loved his sense of humor; we laughed easily together, and I was constantly taken with his intelligence and enthusiasm for all aspects of his project. John had an impressively encyclopedic and reverent knowledge of film history. He would quote lines and scenes effortlessly, as if he'd somehow had the time to study two-dozen great or even obscure movies the night before, and every night before that. His mind was vast and rife with quick references to every genre of the art form. Not only did he know what he wanted to see on screen, but he had a keen theatrical approach which became a shorthand between us, calling upon our similar backgrounds. His knowledge of and love for music was also a common link for us. We talked about and shared musical quotes quite often. And to say that John's storyboards were detailed would be an understatement. His hand-drawn work was not only artistic, but incredibly nuanced with a distinct point of view; quite often a cleverly unexpected humor or irony.*

Black Roses Demon makeup

John welcomed me into the Fasano Family Troupe, and I greatly enjoyed getting to know so many of the close circle that surrounded him and his vision. For a young actor John's circle was a comfy safety net over which to confidently dive into, creating HIS vision. His "can-do" style was infectious. Loyally supporting and sharing John's mission were his talented literary-minded wife Cindy, of course, always protective, and warmly maternal to us all, his always optimistic and watchful sister Felicia Fasano, who cheerfully with her make-up skills, kept me (and all) looking fresh, or scary, as the scenes dictated, and his trusted and vastly talented buddies Frank Dietz, Tony Bua, and Richie Alonzo. Each so talented and committed to John's focused and buoyant vision. Like so many others that worked on and supported BR; great folks and definitely part of the Fasano Family magic. The proposed shooting schedule of **Black Roses** *up in Toronto conflicted with the Broadway transfer and opening of a new musical in which I had been playing the male lead for over two years, during its development, backers' auditions, and Off-Broadway run. John was greatly troubled by the notion that his movie would be costing me this opportunity not to make my Broadway debut (I had done that some years earlier in "The Three Musketeers") but to originate my first leading role in a new Broadway Show. Through much careful negotiation, John was able to arrange the shooting schedule in such a way that I could return to New York in time for the Broadway Opening of "Romance/Romance". The producers of the show, in order to hold my job, asked that I step into the position of standby for the new leading man who would replace me. Not perfect,* D return

to the show, even as an off-stage cover. Scott Bakula stepped-in to open "Romance/Romance", garnering a Tony Award nomination for his work and he was terrific in the show. What ever happened to him? (laughs) A few months later, when it was time for Scott to return to LA for his series, I took over the role. Guess who bought-out an entire row of the Helen Hayes Theatre on my Opening Night? John Fasano. He and his family cheered loudly and proudly as their "Damian" romped and sang his way through a Schnitzler-inspired turn of the century Vienna, and a modern summer share in the Hamptons, in the two acts of the musical, respectively. We all celebrated at the legendary Sardi's Restaurant next-door to the theatre afterwards. It was an evening with the great John Fasano and family that I will never forget. Of course, in addition to **Black Roses***, I was thrilled to join John at his invitation for his next feature film,* **The Jitters***, as well; and to extend the working relationship and our friendship to one that I will always cherish and NEVER get enough of. I only regret that we never made another feature together, as I was and am such a fan of not only his extraordinary talents as a director, but of his humanity, his great vision, his sense of humor, his intelligence, and his wonderful reverence for the art of moviemaking. I learned so much from John. I will always remember his voice, and the youthful exuberance with which he approached all of his projects, and just about any situation in life as well. Gone too soon, John. Thank you, John.*

Obviously both Sal and Frank have done a great deal more than star in the works of John Fasano, even if that is what we horror and exploitation fans best know them for. Sal also shared with us what his "post-Damian" world has been like.

Sal Viviano: *Most of my career has been on the stage, having done extended runs in seven Broadway shows, almost twice as many Off-Broadway, and many other theatrical productions all over the country, including a few national tours. In the last 15 years or so I have also appeared with over 100 symphonic pops orchestras, singing over 300 "themed" concerts of mostly Broadway Hits or songs from The Great American Songbook. In addition, I've recorded on just over 70 CDs, including original cast recordings, compilations, and movie soundtracks. My wife of 20 years is the exceptionally versatile actress Liz Larsen, currently co-starring as Genie Klein in "Beautiful" The Carole King Musical, on Broadway. We have two teenage sons, of whom we are so proud. Alessandro Gian, and Joseph Dante. We play a lot of sports together, and I had, as recently as this summer even, the great pleasure of coaching each of them at different times, both in basketball and baseball. We live in New York City, and also have a home in Los Angeles.*

I know that I am lucky to have gotten to know John Fasano in the last few years and from the words and stories shared by both Frank and Sal it would seem that anyone who was lucky enough to get to know John was a better person for it. I close by saying thank you, John. I have been a fan of yours since I was 11 years old and it will be my honor and pleasure to continue to fly the flag for you, your art, your passion, and your talents in the days and years to come. One of a kind, John. We love you, we'll miss you.

REMEMBERING OX BAKER

Douglas 'Ox" Baker was a professional wrestler. He was trained by Buddy Austin, Pat O'Conner, and Bob Geigel. He made his debut in 1964 and was initially a "baby face." He soon turned "heel" as he was a natural ring villain with a shaved head, bushy Fu Manchu mustache, and his booming voice. His finishing move was "The Heartpunch," where he would punch his opponent over the heart causing the heart to "stop" and allow the pin fall. The move was "borrowed" from Stan Stasiak, who was pissed about Baker using it. Baker changed the move to "The Heart Crusher." Stasiak and Baker squared off down the road in Texas for a Heart Punch vs. Heart Punch match which Stasiak won.

Ox worked for the WWWF as "The Friendly Arkansas Ox" in 1967. Then worked for just about every major and minor promotion worldwide. I started watching wrestling in the '70s. I knew about Ox from reading the fake wrestling magazines at the time. I say fake because everything was "akefay" back then. The business was never exposed as it has been today. Strange thing I did read that Ox had killed two men in the ring. He was a scary guy for sure.

In the '70s Ox joined the International Wrestling Association. Run by White Sox owner Eddie Einhorn and Pedro Martinez, IWA was going to give the WWWF competition. It had a midnight TV slot on Saturday nights on NY's WOR Channel 9. Its roster was a who's who of stars. Mil Mascaras was the champ. Ernie Ladd, Ivan Koloff, Dick "The Bulldog" Brower, Eric the Red, The Love Brothers, The Islanders (Wild Samoans), The Mighty Igor, Lars Anderson, and others were the major players. But even back then, the WWWF had huge clout and wasn't going allow the IWA to get a foothold on the East Coast.

IWA was frozen out of any venue that the WWWF ran in. This limited their East Coast shows to the decaying Roosevelt Stadium in Jersey City. They ran shows in Buffalo, NY, Cleveland, Ohio, and a couple of other venues. During this time Ox was in a feud with Ernie Ladd. This feud caused a riot in Cleveland as Ox nailed Ladd with a heart punch and kept on punching him until the crowd tried to storm the ring.

Eventually the IWA folded, and a lot of its wrestlers were blacklisted. Wrestling promoters operated like the Mafia back then. Because the IWA dared to encroach on Vince McMahon Sr.'s territory, the wrestlers involved were punished. A lot of them, including Ox, went to Japan, Australia, and New Zealand. Others worked for "renegade" promotions just to stay solvent. It was hard to find work when you got blackballed.

When one of the greatest wrestlers of all times, Bruno Sammartino, got vocal about how he was being used, he was set up for a blackball. He was booked in two places on the same date. Missing one booking warranted a blackball. But Bruno was shrewd and contacted a promoter in Toronto, Canada. Bruno knew that he would appeal to the Italian population there. His gamble paid off and when Vince asked him to return Bruno had one condition, he wanted the belt off of then champion, Nature Boy Buddy Rogers. Rogers had a penchant for purposely injuring opponents and Bruno despised him for it. Bruno beat him in record time, breaking Roger's back in the process.

In 1971, Ox was wrestling for the American Wrestling Association. During a tag match with Baker and "The Claw" against Alberto Torres and "Cowboy" Bob Ellis, Torres was injured during the match and died three days later. His death was blamed on Baker's heart punch. Truth was that Torres had injured his pancreas before this match and that was the real cause of his death.

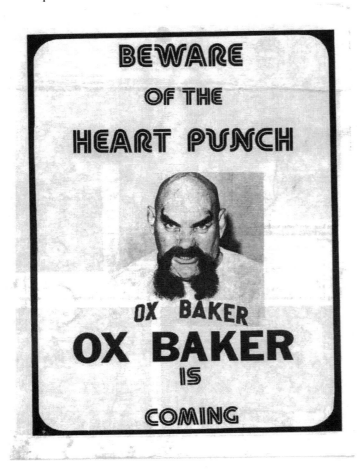

In 1972, Ox was wrestling promoter/wrestler Ray Gunkel. Gunkel won the match, but collapsed in the locker room dead from a heart attack. Ox was now getting billed as "Killer" Ox Baker. This really bothered Ox. In an interview a couple of years ago, Ox explained that Gunkel went to an all you can eat fried chicken place before the show. His over indulgence, then getting into the ring right after eating, gave him the heart attack.

Ox returned to the WWWF supposedly for a program with then-champion, Bob Backlund. He was on WWWF TV twice, managed by The Grand Wizard of Wrestling, Ernie Roth. I looked forward to seeing Ox in action, but it never happened. For whatever reason, he was never used. I saw him soon after on the Spanish network that ran Lucha Libre from the Olympic Auditorium in Los Angles. He teamed with The "Enforcer" Luciano, a one-eyed wrestler. In 1989, he opened Ox Baker's Wrestling School in Connecticut. Some of his graduates were Bryan Clark (Adam Bomb), Mark Calaway (The Undertaker), Bulldog Blanski, and others.

Ox also started to appear in some movies. He was in Jackie Chan's *The Big Brawl* (1980) and *Escape from New York* (1981). In *Escape from New York*, he was Kurt Russell's opponent, Slag, in a fight to the death. Russell said in an interview that Ox was getting a tad rougher than he should have during that scene. Kurt said he had to tap Ox "in the balls" a couple of times with his bat to get him to calm down.

In 1990 I was asked to work security for a convention called Horrorthon. This convention would become Chiller Theater. Ox Baker was to be one of the guests. Only having read about Ox, I didn't know what to expect. He was brought in by a guy called Big Andy. Andy worked security for Vince Sr. and knew a lot of the wrestlers. This was a two day show, held in a rundown movie theater in Rutherford NJ.

Andy introduced me to Ox, who looked scary. Later I was asked to tell people there was no smoking in the building. As I walked up to Andy, I saw Ox lighting his pipe. I said to Andy that there's no smoking in here. I saw Ox cock an eyebrow at that, so I quickly said, "Don't worry, Ox, I got you covered." He grabbed me in a bear hug and said, "Thanks buddy." We were having a charity auction and I asked Ox if he would put something in the auction. He stood up, took his chair and twisted it into a knot. I stood there, dumbfounded. He took my sharpie and wrote "I broke it, Ox Baker" on the chair and handed it to me. About an hour later he was bellowing about something. The promoter asked me to take away his mike. I said, "He doesn't have a mike. That's just him taking."

Now I go down the road a few years. I was working for NYC Liquidators. Leaving work one day, who do I see standing on the corner of my block but Ox Baker himself. He was selling stuff, "Wacky Packs," out of his car. I found out that he just beat colon cancer. He wasn't doing well money-wise then. Feeling bad for him, I called Kevin Clement of Chiller Theater. I told him what I knew and Kevin said he'd give him a table at the next show.

Ox came in and took up three tables. I had to explain that he only had one. He was in rare form, terrorizing people and loving it. He walked through the lobby after the show bellowing, "Why are you people smoking in here?" Then he said, "I think I just shit my pants," and went to his room. He did appear at a few more Chiller Conventions.

In the later years, Ox would make sporadic appearances for some indie promotions. He confronted Dusty Rhodes at a Ring of Honor show. He was in Combat Zone Wrestling as part of Halfbreed Billy Gram's Cult Fiction stable. Wrestler Toby Klein told me that even in his advanced age Ox was still a very tough man. He was a surprise entrant in a 13-man Battle Royal in Cleveland in 2013. A few years before that he and Killer Kowalski won a tag team title in New England.

On October 20th, 2014, Ox passed away at age 80 after a heart attack. It was sad news for me and many other fans. Despite his ferocious appearance, Ox was a sensitive guy and a good person. It's just sad that he was overlooked by the WWWF where he could have been a killer heel and probably would have had a program with Hulk Hogan down the road. RIP Doug "Ox" Baker.

12 HOURS ON "THE DEUCE" REVISITED
THE BICENTENIAL YEAR 1976

By 42 St. Pete

Seems a lot of you readers like stories of my prowling around 42nd Street in all its scuzzy glory. Let me take you back to another lost Saturday night, this time during the 200th birthday of our country, The Bicentennial Celebration. You had the longships in the harbor, security was really tight, and because of that there was no fuckin' weed coming into the country. None, nada—it was the great pot famine of '76. Yes, back then we could secure our borders.

While it was a dry summer in the city, there *was* hashish—lots of it. It seemed that a shipment of butcher block tables wasn't made of butcher block, they were made of hashish. By the end of '76 I was so sick of smoking that crap that I never indulged it again. But Saturday night was party night and the party was in NYC. I was hanging out with two friends, Jimmy and Ian. Jimmy was a fat, lazy bastard who worked the graveyard shift at a place that made doughnuts. After visiting him at work one night and seeing this big, nasty machine that spit out greasy pastries, I lost my taste for doughnuts for a while.

Ian was a skinny guy who'd moved here from Great Britain. He had a "real job" and Jimmy would leach off him for money and weed. Jimmy never had money; we would go to a movie and he would announce he was broke when we got there. So it was either take him home or pay his way in. He didn't pull this shit with me. We were going to a Drive-In when he pulled the 'no money' trick. Instead of paying his way I made him get into the trunk. He bitched about being claustrophobic, but I told him no one was paying and he could walk home. He got in and I made sure I hit every bump in the Drive-In at 30 MPH. He never tried the 'no money' crap with me again.

This Saturday was Jimmy's birthday and he wanted to go to a peepshow. Each of us had a vehicle. I had a tricked-out van with a flaming skull on the hood, coiled snakes on the side, and jacked-up chrome wheels. My truck drew a lot of attention. Sometimes the wrong kind of attention. Jimmy had a plain van and Ian had a Toyota. Whoever had the most gas was going to drive. Jimmy's truck had the almost-full tank, so he drove. The cheap bastard wasn't too happy about burning *his* gas for a change.

It was around 7pm when we paid the $1.50 toll at the Lincoln Tunnel. We cruised down 8th avenue, then up 42nd Street. The marquees were lit up in a bright neon glow. The block was packed with hookers hanging out in front of porn theaters and bookstores until the cops rousted them. 'Beat' drug salesmen offered coke (baking powder), nickel bags (oregano), and acid. Male hustlers stood outside of Blackjack Books trying to make "movie money." We were looking for a parking space as Jimmy didn't want to pay to park in a lot.

We drove up and down the streets and found nothing. Then one pass down 40th street, damn, we actually found a space. Not the safest place to park, but finding a parking space in this area on a Saturday night was like finding a hooker who was a virgin. Securing the van, we walked down 40th street to 8th Avenue. We walked past a row of shoe shine stands run by old black hustlers. The stands sold bottles of cheap wine after the liquor stores closed. We walked past the decrepit Anco Theater right on the corner of 8th and 42nd. Once an exploitation and sexploitation grinder, The Anco was a rip-off artist's wet dream as you could rob someone, duck into The Anco, run out the exit into an alley that connected all the theaters on that side of the block. The thief would just run into an exit for another theater and vanish. The Anco was showing double bills of porn at this time.

Turning the corner, we walked past the store that sold fake IDs, police badges, and weapons. A black guy was standing in front of Athena Liquors yelling "loose joints." He was rousted by the owner, a Greek woman who would take no shit and kept a loaded .38 close at hand. I found later that she was the aunt of a good friend of mine. We kept on strolling and working on our neon tans. Past The Victory, The Liberty, The Rialto, and the other grindhouses. We were on the corner of 42nd and 7th avenue, not a real safe place to be. The New Amsterdam was the last grindhouse on the right side of the block. You had Topp's Bar, a great place to get in trouble if you were stupid enough to venture in. You passed The New Barracks, a gay 'bath house' that attracted black gay hustlers and leather 'toughs'. It was the most dangerous spot on The Deuce, but three guys as big and ugly as us were rarely approached by anyone.

There was an island between 7th avenue and Broadway. Right on that island was a dirty white building. We called it The Porno Super Market. Its real name was Crossroads Books. If you ever saw the Nic Cage film called *8mm*, there was a scene in a porn place that had all kinds of illegal stuff. That was Crossroads Books. The place was a real den of iniquity. Music played loudly as we checked out the endless rows of peep booths. Big hand-written signs were posted over each booth. Any perverted sex act known to man was available to view for a mere 25 cents. "See the Barbra Streisand Blow Job Movie," "*White Girl with Black Dog,*" "*Girl with Pig, Oink, Oink,*" pissing, shitting, bondage, torture, and the one that stopped us in our tracks. *Snuff: the Bloodiest Film on 42nd Street.*

This wasn't the Roberta and Michael Findley film; this was an 8mm loop. Stoned and intrigued, as these "snuff" films had made the news, we decided to see it. The three of us squeezed into the booth, which was frowned upon by management but no one saw us. The first quarter triggered the projector. A woman was being whipped and blood was running down her back. Another quarter and now the girl was getting slapped around and beaten. Quarter #3 had a guy pull out a serrated knife, stick it in her pussy, and started sawing. Blood spurted, flesh parted, and Ian turned green and left. Jimmy followed a minute later. I didn't go any further as I had been an apprentice butcher after high school. I knew raw meat when I saw it and this was raw meat.

Over time, people have said the films were a hoax. It seems the Catholic Church were the ones spreading the snuff rumor. According to David Friedman fake snuff films were made to cash in on the rumor. The "effects" were supposedly more amateurish than *Blood Feast*. I never saw those films, only this one and from where I stood, it was real. Crossroads Books was eventually shut down by the city. Urban legend said that anti-porn people fire bombed it, but that's bullshit. The place had taken things too far and had to go. It was closed as part of a "deal" the city made. Make no mistake about it, the mob controlled the sex trade in Times Square. Bookstores, mini cinemas, massage parlors, and higher priced "leisure" spas were all mob controlled. Every so often, things got out of hand like Crossroads. The deal included a short-stay hooker hotel and a low-end strip bar that had to go too.

Now it was around 9:30pm and those two were done, they wanted to go home. I didn't. My "the night is still young" didn't work. They were going across the river. I wasn't, and I kept a little stash of cash for these lost weekends. So Ian and Jimmy left me at Crossroads Books. Fine, I decided to check out the dancers in a peep-o-rama booth. Low-rent skanks grappling for tips. These were windowless peeps, meaning girls would let you suck a tit, lick a pussy, or eat an ass for tips. Nothing more hygienic than sucking a spit-slobbered boob. Not this guy. Looking up, I saw that security was just a guy sitting on a bar stool with a sawed off shotgun. I left for the safer confines of my favorite watering hole, Club 44 on West 44th street.

I had been frequenting this place since 1969 when I was 16. It was a loud dive type bar with bikini clad barmaids and bouncer/doorman, ex-boxer Nino Valdez. Nino was built like a refrigerator. He took no shit but was a cool guy once you got to know him. Once when a bunch of us got a little rowdy, Candy, one of the barmaids, told us "Nino is buying this round." Translated, this gesture meant we were close to crossing the line, so here's your pass, drink up, and leave. We did just that and thanked him for the drink. I always respected the big guy.

It was about 10:30 pm when I got there. I shook hands with Nino then ordered a Michelob. Different conversations were taking place. Some guys were bitching about the Yankees. One guy was talking about the *Ilsa* double feature at The Apollo. An obvious streetwalker was bitching about the influx of out-of-town whores that had come to NYC to cash in on the Bicentennial celebrations. Nino usually wouldn't allow working girls to hang out in the bar. Being that all this one was doing was bitching, and not approaching anyone, he didn't toss her. She was drunk and entertaining. She was telling a story about a guy from Jersey that wanted to do "Greek" with her in his car. Seems the steering wheel got in the way.

Talk turned to the new place on the corner of 42nd and 8th, Show World Center. It was a four-floor porn emporium with a

bookstore, rows of peep booths, live nude girls, and live sex shows. It was built on the sneak starting in 1974, and had just opened a few months ago. It was all chrome, linoleum, and flashing neon. Pulsing music played as change barkers hawked the live peeps and sex shows. It was a carnival atmosphere; it was actually clean and had visible security. Taking a page from The Melody Burlesque, Show World booked name porn stars for its Triple Treat Theater. Prior to Show World opening, most of the peepshows and bookstores were filthy. Peep booths had a shower curtain over them. Some were just out in the open, old film machines that used to show boxing matches through a viewer were converted to porn. Some places had a row of peeps that were always broken. Other places, like 250 Book Center on 42nd Street, had their machines in the back of the store where gay men cruised each other.

Show World actually elevated the area. Why go into a piss-smelling sinkhole while Show World provided a safe, secure place to rub one out? Chronic masturbators flocked to Show World in droves. Porn star Samantha Fox was the featured attraction for the weekend. I decided to check it out. I walked back down 44th to 8th Avenue and passed a group of frat boys being hustled by two black dudes. The black guys claimed to have a truck load of TVs "just down the block." "Sonys," he said, "just $75 each." One guy seemed interested. "Jest gimme the cash and I'll be right back." The moron actually gave up the money. Odds are he's still there waiting for his

hot TV.

Show World had two entrances: one on 42nd Street through its small but well-stocked book and sex toy shop, or the main entrance on 8th Avenue. It was about 11:45 pm when I entered the place. The live show had been $7, but was raised to $10 for this momentous Samantha Fox occasion. The Triple Threat Theater was a stage against a wall with rows of folding chairs on the three sides surrounding it. I took a seat up front as a listless, 'luded out stripper finished her "act." The bank of TVs over the stage lit up with Swedish erotica loops playing. The aroma of Pinesol permeated the air.

Finally the MC, porn star Bobby Astyr, announced Ms. Fox. Samantha came out and did a striptease. She tossed her panties to a group of old men who devoured them. She got down to the buff, flashed some pussy, and it was over. A whole fifteen minutes. An old man muttered, "This is bullshit." I had to agree. Now the loops were playing again. I figured I'd stick around and get my money's worth. A "Love Team" came out to perform. Nasty, fat, and sweaty with a hairy back. The guy was pretty bad too. After about five minutes of nothing, I left. Back out on 8th Avenue, it was about 1 am. I decided to take in a movie.

First I went to Athena Liquors for a pint that I could bring in. No one questioned you back then. You'd be watching a movie and you would keep hearing the sound of empty bottles and cans hitting the floor. There were 15 theaters on "The Deuce" between 8th Avenue and Broadway. Seven were owned by The Brandt Organization: The Liberty, The Victory, The Apollo, The Lyric, The Empire, The Times Square, and The Selwyn. The Brandt's got them though bank foreclosures during the Great Depression. The Victory was their only porn house. The Brandts kept the ticket prices lower than other theaters running the same films. That ensured packed houses every weekend. The Double Bills were astounding: *Dirty Harry* and *Magnum Force*; *The Texas Chainsaw Massacre* and *Torso*; *Snuff* and *The Devil's Nightmare*; *Five Fingers of Death* and *Queen Boxer*; *Assault on Precinct 13* and *Kid Vengeance*; *Legend of Nigger Charlie* and *Soul of Nigger Charlie*. I opted for *The Texas Chainsaw Massacre* and *Torso* at The Rialto.

The main feature, *Chainsaw Massacre*, started at 1:30 am. *Torso* had about 10 minutes left before it ran out. I noticed on the one sheets that Joseph Brenner has released *Torso* and Bryanston Pictures released *Chainsaw*. Brenner's company specialized in violent European films. He released Umberto Lenzi's pivotal cannibal film, *Deep River Savages* as *Man From Deep River*. He also released *Eyeball, Shock Waves*, The *Ginger* films, and *Almost Human* before calling it quits in the mid '80s. Bryanston was run by the Perainos, who produced and distributed *Deep Throat, Devil in Miss Jones,* and other porn. True to form, no one was paid as the Perainos used Bryanston as a tax dodge. Eventually "Big Tony" Peraino went to jail and a hit was put out on his brother Joseph and a nephew.

TCM opened with narration over a pile of bones. Several people had obviously seen it already and were making pig-snorting noises a few rows behind me. The crowd popped every time Leatherface claimed a victim. They hooted and cheered as Franklin was cut up in his wheelchair.

Nothing was like a 42nd Street audience as they really got into these films. By the time Sally got away I had sucked my pint of hooch dry and had to piss during the end credits. The Rialto, as well as most of the other theaters, was closing and it was about 3 am. I was going to take a bus back and call it a night. I went to Port Authority and found out that some drunk frat boy had decided to play demolition derby on the way out of the self-parking lot and had flipped his muscle car over. This blocked the way out as he had made it almost to the ramp leading to the Lincoln Tunnel. Pissed off, I headed back to Club 44 for a nightcap.

The place was pretty dead. "Bad night?" Nino asked. I told him about the auto thrill show. They said it would be a couple of hours before it was clear. Last call was at 4 am. I nursed that last drink until 4:30 am. Now my choices were limited. The Harem was a porn grinder that was open 24/7 with triple and quadruple bills of porn. It was inhabited by sleepers, drag queens, pre-op trannies, $5 hookers, and

18

some freaks that defied description. No fuckin' way was I going there. I knew of an afterhours place on the lower east side, but my funds were low. That left The Venus Theater down on 8th Avenue. It was around 5 am, The Venus closed at 7 am and opened at 10 am. I was out of hooch but had one joint that I had saved. So I paid the $3 and went inside.

I looked for a seat away from the flotsam that were either comatosely fucked-up or snoring. I settled in and lit my joint, getting some unwanted attention from some butt-ugly bitch who had to be a tranny. "Pass that doobie over here, honey," it said. I pretended not to hear her. Then she offered to blow me for a hit. I took a hit that burned the joint down to my fingertips then handed her or it what was left. "Take it and leave me the fuck alone." I coughed. She seemed miffed that I didn't want the hummer. On screen John Holmes was banging some hot chick. It was his Johnny Wadd persona. I never liked

Holmes as I'm not into watching a guy with a dick bigger than mine. Then a guy came running up the aisle and out the front door. A middle-aged guy was chasing him. Looked like he cruised the wrong guy and had his wallet lifted. I heard him yelling at the cashier like it was their fault. Security told him to take a seat or leave.

The first film ended and another Holmes film came on, *Flesh of the Lotus*. I had walked into a Johnny Wadd film festival. At 7 am the film stopped and the house lights went on. Sleepers were rousted by security tapping a baseball bat on the back of their seat. "Closing time!" the guy bellowed. I was up and out. I looked at the mess the patrons left behind. Empty cans of Colt.45 and King Cobra, empty Boones Farm and Thunderbird pints, rubbers, tissues, the odd issue of Screw, and empty food containers. I didn't envy the cleanup guys. In two hours The Venus would open again.

People asked me why places like The Venus opened so early. But it wasn't just the porn grinders, most of the movie houses opened early. Why? This was the city that never slept. Third shift workers would go to see a movie after they got off. So it made sense for these places to open early and close late. The wreckage had been cleared up and the buses were running. As I headed back, I was already planning next weekend.

ONCE YOU GO BLACK, YOU'LL NEVER LOOK BACK.
THE BLAXPLOITATION FILMS
By 42P

In the '60s and '70s, there was a lot of racial unrest. There were the Newark Riots, The Watts Riots, etc. There was right and wrong on both sides of the fence. Grindhouses were located in a lot of those areas, especially Newark, New Jersey. Not being a prejudiced person, I didn't give a shit, but common sense had to prevail. Was seeing a movie worth getting beaten up, robbed or stabbed over? No, but danger went with the territory back then.

But people are fuckin' people and people go to the movies. Black folk made up a large audience of movie-goers. Maybe a thought clicked in some studio executive's head that this was a paying audience that should be tapped into. Inadvertently, the first guy who actually grasped this concept was the zombie master himself, George A Romero. Romero cast Duane Jones in the lead for *Night of the Living Dead*. Jones auditioned for the part and was the best man for the job. Romero and company had stated that race had nothing to do with the decision; Jones nailed it and made history.

But this was an indie film in 1968. The studios had already found the guy they felt would draw black audiences to the theaters. Ex-football star Jim Brown was that guy. In 1964 he co-starred with Richard Boone, Stuart Whitman, and Tony Franciosa in the adult themed western, *Rio Conchos*. Brown joined an all-star cast for 1967's *The Dirty Dozen* where he got high marks for his portrayal of Jefferson, a soldier sentenced to death for the murder of a fellow soldier who tried to kill him because of his color. Brown was on a roll. He starred in *The Slams, Tick, Tick, Tick, Dark Of The Sun, The Split, Ice Station Zebra, 100 Rifles,* and *El Condor*. Brown was "the man," but someone was about to raise the bar and piss off a lot of people at the same time.

Melvin Van Peebles wrote, produced, directed, and scored *Sweet Sweetback's Baadasss Song* (1971), a scathing indictment of white America. "Rated X by an All-White Jury," the print ads screamed. "You Bled My Mama, You Bled My Poppa, But You Won't Bleed Me," the one sheet poster proclaimed. "The Film that THE MAN Doesn't Want You to See." Van Peebles had previously directed *The Watermelon Man* for Columbia. He took the money he made from that film, about $70,000, and used it to make *Sweetback*.

Van Peebles created more than controversy with this film. *Sweetback* was the most successful independent film ever made at this time. Shot from a black man's POV, we see how Sweetback is screwed over by crooked white cops and the system. Sweetback plays along for a while, but when he sees cops beating down a young black guy for no reason, he goes righteously postal. Cops were assholes to anyone different back then. As a hippie I was constantly harassed, but never to the extent that was showed here. Over 40 years later, not much has changed as far as cops and the black man. Sweetback gets revenge in an orgy of brutal violence and the crowd loved him for it.

Things weren't all hearts and flowers though. No company would distribute *Sweetback*. Enter exploitation czar Jerry Gross, whose company, Cinemation, was in Chapter 11. Jerry was smart enough to know this film would be a money maker. He cut a deal that insured Van Peebles a big payday. But *Time, Newsweek,* the *NY Times,* and most other mainstream publications refused to even review the film. Van Peebles decided he had to be up in their faces and keep in their faces. Since he couldn't count on the mainstream media to do shit for him, he wouldn't pander to them. Word of mouth was the best review and people were talking. This was the birth of the Blaxploitation film.

Now the studios knew that they could cast a strong, maybe militant, black actor in a lead role. They had their actor, Jim Brown. *Slaughter* (1972) was the film. Slaughter is an ex-Green Beret out to avenge the

deaths of loved ones at the hands of the mob. Jack Starrett directed, and the movie co-starred Rip Torn, Cameron Michell, and Connie Stevens. *Slaughter* was a big hit. *Black Gunn* was next with a similar plot. Brown is a nightclub owner whose brother steals some money and, more importantly, ledger books from the mob. When the mob takes out his brother Big Jim goes out for revenge. Veteran character actors Bruce Glover and Martin Landau are the bad guys. *Slaughter* warranted a sequel, so in 1973 we got *Slaughter's Big Ripoff*. The big casting coup here was *Tonight Show* co-host, Ed McMahon, as a heavy. Co-stars were Gloria Hendry and Don Stroud.

About this time porn was going mainstream, former professional boxer Johnny Keyes was paired with Marilyn Chambers in *Behind the Green Door*. That film drew a large black audience. The light bulb went off in the low-rent porn filmmakers minds that interracial fucking would sell. Movies, one-day wonders, were shot on the cheap with black guys banging white girls as a selling point. Films like *Black Neighbors, Up at J.J.'s Place, Black Lovers*, and more made the rounds of the inner city porn grinders. The films featured a largely unattractive cast, usually a bunch of black dudes and an overweight blonde girl. Keyes returned in *The Resurrection of Eve, Sex World, Pro Ball Cheerleaders*, all bigger-budgeted high-profile films. Today black porn has become an industry onto itself.

Another high profile film that followed on the heels of *Sweetback* was *Shaft* (1971), based on the novel by Ernest Tidyman. Richard Roundtree made the role his own. Prior to *Shaft*, Roundtree was in the Allan Funt film *What Do You Say To a Naked Lady? Shaft* had a bigger budget and benefited from New York locations. Shaft is a street-smart detective who has to rescue the kidnapped daughter of a Harlem Mob King Pin. One of the best detective movies of the '70s, the film won an Oscar for Issac Hayes' soundtrack. This was a "Blaxploitation" film that drew in mainstream audiences.

Fred Williamson was another pro football player turned actor. After doing some TV work, he was cast as Captain Oliver "Spear-Chucker" Jones in *M*A*S*H*. After that, he was given the lead roles in *The Legend of Nigger Charley* and *Hammer*, both in 1972. *Charley* is a low budget western, with Williamson as a former slave heading west. It might have been made to capitalize on *Roots* which was hot at the time. The plot of *Charley* (as well as the premise of the James Garner/Lou Gossett Jr. team-up, *The Skin Game*) was "borrowed" by Quentin Tarantino for *Django Unchained*.

Hammer was a different story. Fred plays a dock worker-turned-prize fighter. He has a crooked manager who is also a drug dealer. Fred is told to take a dive and his girlfriend is kidnapped to ensure he does. After this film, Fred was forevermore nicknamed "The Hammer."

Next, Fred would get the role which would define his career. *Black Caesar* (1973) was written and directed by street-smart NYC native, Larry Cohen. Fred was cast as Tommy Gibb. Tommy has criminal aspirations because, as a boy, he had his leg broken by a cop on the take. Laid up in the hospital, he seethes with anger at what's going on around him. Nursing his anger, he rises to power in the Harlem underworld. He finds power the solution to his vengeance. He does a freelance hit to curry favor with the Mob. Reluctantly accepted, he becomes more aggressive, breaking away and starting a gang war. *Black Caesar* was a huge hit, especially with the inner city audiences who could identify with the characters. The film also benefited from a James Brown soundtrack. Cohen was savvy enough to use both blacks and whites as bad guys instead of the "token" white bad guy.

Black moviegoers, especially on "The Deuce," identified with these characters. Hell, they did business there and real life and death situations went down between black street hustlers and the Mob. The Mob controlled all of the porn, massage parlors, and sex related businesses in NYC. They stayed away from street prostitution as they felt pimps were too stupid to deal with. But when a couple of pimps opened competing massage parlors, they were fire bombed out of existence.

If you're up on mob history, the old timers, known as Mustache Petes, were strongly opposed to selling drugs. The young up-and-comers knew that drugs were the future, so the old guard was eliminated. The Mob needed the blacks to sell their shit, so uneasy alliances were formed. These real life scenarios became Blaxploitation movie plots: The Evil Wops vs. The Brothers. Of course *Black Caesar* was so popular that it warranted a sequel, *Hell Up in Harlem* (1973). Seems Tommy Gibbs was only wounded, not killed, in the first film. Larry Cohen again directed. Tommy is a man won't go down without a fight. He has a bunch of ledgers with the names of all the corrupt officials, payoffs, and the like. Not as good as the original since Cohen used a double in some scenes as Fred had prior commitments. Fred's close ups were shot out in Los Angeles where he was now based. Most of the film was shot in New York using the same crew that was used on Cohen's monster movie, *It's Alive*.

Fred was a take charge kind of guy. He grabbed the director's chair for *Mean Johnny Barrows*. He kept the chair and was his own star. In 1978 Fred was cast in *Inglorious Bastards*, an *Italian Dirty Dozen* knockoff. Directed by Enzo Castellari, it became a cult favorite. Williamson knew he would be a big hit overseas. He stayed in Italy, doing a bunch of films there and in other European locals.

Warner Brothers, who were impressed by the success of *Shaft*, decided they wanted to enter this genre of films. They gave *Superfly (1972)* the green light. *Superfly* was the film that broke down the barriers of what a drug dealer was supposed to be. Ron O'Neal played Superfly to perfection. The tagline, "He Has a Plan to Stick it to the Man," was his mantra. The Man was the establishment and, for the first time, the drug dealer didn't get his comeuppance in the end. He became the one to hand it out. The film had a huge influence on fashion and music back then. Curtis Mayfield hated the theme of the film and wasn't going to do the soundtrack. Then he realized he could counteract the theme of the movie by writing positive lyrics for the audience to hear. This only made the film more popular.

These films opened the doors for a lot of black actors. Guys that had been used, previously, as thugs, pimps, and winos were getting a lot of work in these films. Oh, they might be cast in the same roles, but now it was different. Actors like John Amos, Raymond Saint Jacques, Godfrey Cambridge, Bernie Casey, Antonio Fargas, Richard Prior, Max Julian, Yaphet Katto, and even Redd Foxx all got work in these films. It is worth noting, historically, that Woody Strode, after getting a lead role in *The Professionals* (1966), was the first black superstar. He had high profile roles in several films and was a favorite of director John Ford. He formed a close friendship with co-star Lee Marvin, who advised him to wear only a vest on the set. Strode was gifted with a phenomenal physic, and stood out among the four leads in the film. After this, Strode was in huge demand overseas, getting cast in spaghetti westerns and crime thrillers. Blaxploitation films had a lot of Kings, but it needed a Queen. Enter Pam Grier.

Pam was working for American International Pictures as a secretary. Roger Corman cast her in two Women-In-Prison films that were to be shot in the Philippines, *Women in Cages* and *The Big Doll House* both in '71. In *Women in Cages* Pam played a sadistic warden. In *the Big Doll House* she played an inmate and was paired with her perennial co-star, Sid Haig. Jack Hill was the director and would go on to direct her biggest hits. AIP honcho, Sam Arkoff, was so impressed with her that he signed her to a five-year contract.

Pam continued working in the Philippines with almost fatal consequences. She contracted a rare tropical disease and almost died. She returned to Los Angeles to do *Cool Breeze*, was then shipped back to the Philippines to do another Jack Hill WIP film, *The Big Bird Cage*. This time she and Sid Haig were "revolutionaries" who stage a prison break to recruit new members. One of the better WIP films, Sid and Pam play off of each other brilliantly. In 1973 Pam tried something different, a horror film called *The Twilight People*. Basically a low budget version of *Island of Lost Souls*, it was directed by Eddie Romero (The *Blood Island* Trilogy). It was also her first time working with actor/producer, John Ashley. Pam *was* "The Panther Woman".

Her last Philippino film would be *Black Mama, White Mama*, again directed by Romero. The film was a low budget remake of *The Defiant Ones* with Pam handcuffed to blonde Margret Markoff. Sid Haig co-starred again. Pam was paired with Margret again for the Italian-lensed epic, *The Arena*. Markoff married actor/producer Mark Damon and left the business. It was back to the States for Pam and another film for Jack Hill. This film would make Pam a legend.

Coffey (1973) was Pam's first starring role. Coffey is a nurse whose sister is hooked on drugs and has her mind destroyed. Coffey haunts the night club scene looking for those responsible. She finds that a pimp, a mobster, the cops, and a well-heeled politician are responsible. Coffey joins the pimp's stable to get information. Lead 'ho, Linda Hayes (*Rolling Thunder*), isn't happy about this and attacks her. But Coffey stuffed her "fro" with razor blades and Linda's hands are shredded. Coffey also uses a can of cheap hairspray and a lighter as a makeshift flame thrower.

Hill did something similar with *Coffey* to what Larry Cohen did with *Black Caesar*. He didn't go with the usual "whites are the bad guys" scenario. Coffey finds out in the end that the people she really trusted were the worst of the worst. *WIP* co-star, Sid Haig plays a henchman called Omar who winds up with a severed jugular, courtesy of Coffey. Pam showed that she could kick major ass and didn't need a man's help. Pam was every white boy's fantasy: a hot, black woman who took no shit.

Pam followed *Coffey* with a series of films directed by a who's who of exploitation directors. *Foxy Brown* (1974 by Jack Hill), *Sheba, Baby* ('75 by William Girdler), *Bucktown* and *Friday Foster* (still '75 by Arthur Marks). She was in *Drum, Greased Lightning, Roots: The Next Generation,* and others. In 1988, Pam was diagnosed with breast cancer and given eighteen months to live. She beat it and plunged back into film and television work. Quentin Tarantino showcased her talents in *Jackie Brown*. She did two films for John Carpenter, *Escape from LA* and *Ghosts of Mars.*

Now, to change the subject a bit, people might wonder how it was to see these films with a predominantly black audience. As I had said, I never gave a shit about a person's race, but some people did. I had two rather nerve-wracking experiences. *Fight for Your Life,* 1977, was a film I should have never gone to see. Released by

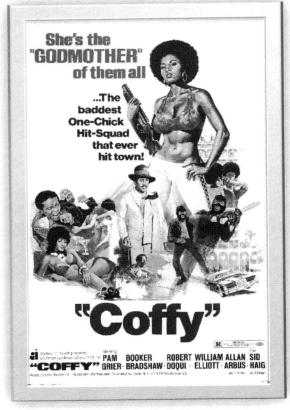

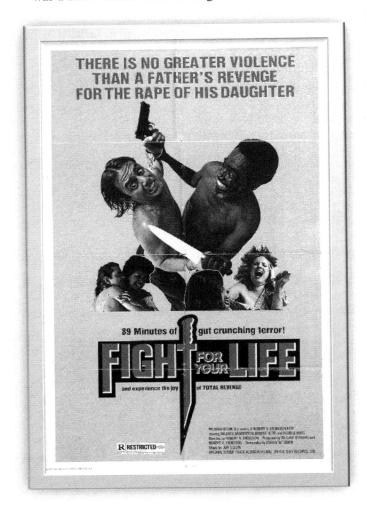

William Mishkin, it was about a group of three cons, led by Jesse Lee Kane (*Newhart*'s William Sanderson in a role I'm sure isn't on his resume), leads a home invasion of a black preacher's family. The film is a racist's wet dream. The trio rape the preacher's daughter, then abuse and debase the rest of his family. The tension in the theater was so thick that you could feel it pulsing. With every racist comment Kane spit out, the crowd got more pissed off. Discretion being the better part of valor, I jetted out before the credits rolled.

At a double bill of *Savage Sisters* and *Blacula* at a theater called The Ormont, I had another near miss. *Savage Sisters* was on first. When it ended the house lights came on. Everyone there turned around and gave me the fisheye. Why the lights came on is a mystery as grindhouses usually didn't have intermissions. Sensing a lot of hostility, I left before anything went down. Usually people tended to mind their own business, but after decades of movie-going, these are the only two incidents that I experienced.

One film that exposed a raw nerve and was quickly pulled from theaters was *Goodbye, Uncle Tom*. Shot in Haiti by the folks who gave us *Mondo Cane 1 & 2*, and *Africa Addido* (U.S title *Africa Blood and Guts*), *Goodbye, Uncle Tom* was a pseudo-documentary about slavery in America in the 1800s. The film crew was given *carte blanche* by Haitian dictator "Papa Doc" Duvalier and made one of the most repulsive, hate- filled films ever. Theaters, faced with the ugly prospect of being trashed by an enraged inner city audience, refused to run the film. Cannon, its distributor, denied that they ever had the film. The film managed to even offend yours truly. It has since been released uncut on DVD by Blue Underground.

Horror films were always popular with lack audiences. So it was inevitable that someone would make a black themed horror film. *Blacula*, 1972, was the first. Classically trained actor, William Marshall, was an African Prince bitten by Count Dracula. Years later, two antique dealers buy some artifacts from Dracula's castle. One of those items is a coffin with Blacula in it. He gets out and feeds on the two dealers. Blacula creates a reign of terror with a small army of vampires in Los Angeles. *Blacula* was a big hit and its sequel, *Scream, Blacula, Scream*, added Pam Grier as a voodoo queen.

As successful as *Blacula* was, other forays into black horror quickly hit the wall. *Abby* 1974, directed by William Girdler, was pulled from distribution when Warner Brothers filled a cease and desist order over similarities to *The Exorcist*. 1973's *Blackenstein* was AIP's 100th film and flopped horribly. It

may have been the worst film ever released in the company's history. The title creature looked like a cross between Herman Munster and Magilla Gorilla. Needless to say, the audience stayed away in droves. Better films were *Horror High, J.D.'s Revenge, Sugar Hill* and her Zombie Hitman, and *Dr Black and Mr Hyde* with Bernie Casey in the lead. A ghetto take on the Robert Lewis Stevenson story, Casey is a kind doctor who tries an experimental serum on himself. He becomes an albino like monster whose hatred of pimps, prostitutes, and drug dealers bubbles to the surface. Casey and a solid cast make this one really work.

No piece on Blaxsploitation films would be complete without the mention of the late, great Rudy Ray Moore. Rudy had a stand-up act that pre-dated Richard Pryor and was filthier than Redd Foxx. His 18 "party albums" sold over a million units without the benefit of airplay. His rhyming comedy structure influenced an entire generation of rappers. In 1975, Rudy produced a movie based on his most favorite character, Dolemite. He followed *Dolemite* with *The Human Tornado, Monkey Hustle, Petey Wheatstraw*, and *Disco Godfather*. In 1996, he was in *Violent New Breed* for my good friend, director Todd Sheets. After Blaxploitation started to die out in the '80s, Rudy went back to doing stand-up until his death in 2008.

The Blaxploitation explosion was from 1970 to 1980. Some felt the entire genre was insulting to blacks. Depends on your point of view. For me, it was a learning experience. Aside from the people previously mentioned, there were some really good actors and actresses making their bones then. If nothing else, these films gave black performers their segue into mainstream films. Ossie Davis, Paul Winfield, James Earl Jones, Gloria Hendry, Moses Gunn, and many other talented people finally got the recognition they deserved as performers.

Like any kind of exploitation film, some of these were total shit. *Black Gestapo, The Black Six, Honky, Black Heat*, and *Mean Mother* were sub-par films cashing in on the popularity of the better-made films. Some of the earlier films benefited immensely because of casting distinctive heavies as bad guys. Hard not to be on top of your game when your co-stars are actors like William Smith, Cameron Mitchell, Don Stroud, Lee Van Cleef, Bruce Glover, Michael Pataki or Robert Quarry. Sadly a lot of the major and minor players are no longer with us.

Being that my era was from 1963 to the mid '80s, I saw just about all of these films in a grindhouse or Drive-In. Blaxploitation films were all part of the tapestry of films which made up the grind house and drive in scene for over a decade. There are no more Grindhouses and the handful of Drive-Ins left are all showing mainstream films. The Blaxploitation films, like any of the genre films, still live on via DVD and Blu-Ray today.

TRUCK TURNER
ONE BAD MUTHA FUCKER

Blaxploitation was in full swing in 1974 when Isaac Hayes took on the role of bounty hunter Mac "Truck Turner. Hayes was a multi-talented composer, singer and musician, who won an Academy Award, Best Original Song for a Motion Picture, for "Theme from *Shaft*". Hayes was big, buff, bald and bearded, a great look for any action film. Hayes teamed with Alan Weeks as Truck and Jerry are after a vicious pimp, Leroy "Gator" Johnson (Paul Harris). Gator took off after bondsman, Fogarty (Dick Miller) put up his bail. Knowing what a vicious SOB Gator is—he set one of his lady's hair on fire with a bucket of gasoline—they want a good payoff. They hold Fogarty up for a grand each. They earn it as they spy Gator in his pimpmobile and give chase. Gator leads them on a demolition derby

before wrecking his car and ducking into a bar.

Gator gives the barflies $50 each to stop Truck and Jerry. After Truck and Jerry brawl with them, one of the beat-down drunks mutters, "We shoulda got more money." Great fight as Turner decimates the barflies. Gator hides out with his white trash blonde 'ho. When Truck corners him, Gators comes out shooting. They blow his ass away, but the blonde stabs Jerry in the shoulder with a scissors. Fogarty grudgingly pays them off, but this sets the stage for revenge by Gator's main lady, Dorinda (Nichelle Nichols).

Dorinda is one tough bitch who takes over Gator's stable. She wants Truck dead for killing Gator. She has a meeting with all the pimps, trying to make a deal: get Turner, get some of her stable. She tells a mouthy pimp that, "I haven't sold my pussy since I was 15, now I sell other people's pussy." A far cry from her squeaky clean *Star Trek* image. Harvard Blue (Yaphet Kotto) was Gator's main rival and he's going to take down Truck. Several independent pimps try and die for their troubles. Blue decides to import three professional hit men, and put $20,000 on Turner's head.

They beat the shit out of Turner's bailsman, forcing him to call the very drunk bounty hunter. Turner, in bed with his squeeze, Annie (Annazette Chase) is too smashed to go, so he calls Jerry. Jerry is blown away by Blue's boys. Truck is now out for revenge, but is afraid Annie will be used to get to him. He takes her shopping and gets her arrested for shoplifting as she is safer in jail. Prior to this, the two found their cat dead, courtesy of Blue.

Truck leans on one of Blue's boys, Desmond, who sends Truck into an ambush. Truck is hip to that, and takes out the three hitmen with a shotgun. West Coast Wrestling fans will recognize former wrestler Earl "Mr. Universe" Maynard as one of the hitmen. Blue visits his friend in the hospital, but Blue leads a team of killers and a bloody shoot out goes down. Turner blows the killers away, but Blue takes a young boy hostage. Turner shoots Blue in the leg, forcing him to let go of the boy. Blue limps out of the hospital, but Turner shoots him in the back. Blue makes it to his car and dies behind the wheel.

Turner goes to Dorinda's place and tells her that she is out of business and to leave town. She pulls a gun on him, thinking he won't shoot a woman. Turner blows her away. Turner waits for a pissed off Annie to get released from jail. He tells her they are leaving town to start a new life. She says she won't go, but Turner has a kitten for her and she decides to go with him.

Truck Turner is one of the least PC films of that era. Truck is called a "smelly nigger" by Jerry in the first ten minutes of the film. Nichelle Nichols is delightfully foul mouthed with "motherfucker this" and "motherfucker that". She is the ho's ho, and I'll bet *Star Trek* geeks pretty much shit themselves when they saw her in this film. Hayes plays Turner as a guy with flaws, not as an invincible hero. The supporting cast is great and look for Charles Cyphers in a small role as a drunk. This was director Jonathan Kaplan's fourth film as he had previously directed *Night All Nurses, Student Teachers*, and *The Slams*.

Hayes continued to act, but never took a role like *Truck Turner* again. He was "The Duke" in Carpenter's *Escape from New York*, he did a lot of TV and voice over work. His "Chef" on *South Park* was supposed to be a one-shot deal, but it went over huge. He was part of the show until he quit in 2006 over religious beliefs. He said "as a civil rights activist for 40 years, I can no longer support a show that disrespects those beliefs and practices." True to form, *South Park* crapped all over his character. Hayes passed away after suffering a stroke in 2008 at age 65. He left a huge legacy in both music and film. He left us way too soon.

42P's TOP TWENTY BLAXPLOITATION FILMS

1. *Sweet Sweetback's BaadAsssss Song*. This is the one that put blaxploitation on the map. Only Jerry Gross had the balls to release it though his Cinemation Industries and made indie film history.

2. *Black Caesar*. Fred Williamson became a huge star with this Larry Cohen directed classic.

3. *Coffy*. After doing a lot of WIP films in the Philippines. Pam Grier returned to the states to star in this kick ass film directed by Jack Hill. This film elevated Pam to superstardom

4. *Slaughter*. After getting great props for his role in The Dirty Dozen, Jim Brown got a huge push with this film. It warranted a sequel, *Slaughter's Big Ripoff*.

5. *Legend of Nigger Charlie*. Fred Williamson is an escaped slave who heads west. Oh, you thought Tarantino's *Django* was an original idea? It wasn't.

6. *Dolemite*. Rudy Ray Moore's film based on the character he created, Dolemite. A blend of comedy and violence followed by *The Human Tornado, Disco Godfather* and others.

7. *Blacula*. William Marshall as an African Prince bitten by the Count. Blacula is resurrected in Los Angeles and starts a reign of terror. Too bad the sequel, and other attempts at black horror, flopped miserably.

8. *Black Belt Jones*. After co-starring in *Enter the Dragon*, Jim Kelly got the lead in this film about the mob trying to take over a karate school.

9. *Three the Hard Way*. Jim Kelly, Fred Williamson, and Jim Brown take on white supremacists, including TV's "Dr. Shrinker" (Jay Robinson) who wants to murder all blacks with a serum dumped in the water supply.

10. *Cotton Comes to Harlem*. Based on Chester Himes' novel, Godfrey Cambridge and Raymond St Jacques are legendary tough cops "Coffin Ed" and "Gravedigger Jones" going after a shady "reverend".

11. *Shaft*. Big budget film with an Ernest Tidyman screenplay, shot in NYC and released by MGM. This made Richard Roundtree a star and elevated the blaxploitation film into the mainstream.

12. *Superfly*. One film that had a huge influence on fashion and music. Ron O'Neal is Superfly and "he's got a plan to stick it to the man" that had audience's cheering at the end.

13. *Abby*. Great cast, William Marshall, Austin Stoker, Terry Carter and Carol Speed, but was pulled from distribution when Warner Brother's sued over similarities to their film, *The Exorcist*.

14. *Take a Hard Ride*. Jim Brown, Fred Williamson, and Jim Kelly reunite in this Western epic assisted by Spaghetti Western legend, Lee Van Cleef.

15. *The Spook Who Sat By the Door*. Directed by Ivan Dixon (*Hogan's Heroes*) The CIA hires its first black agent, who turns and trains urban revolutionaries.

16. *Truck Turner*. Issac Hayes is a bounty hunter battling an army of pimps. Nichelle Nichols craps all over her clean cut Star trek image as a foul mouthed lady pimp.

17. *Slaves*. Ossie Davis and Dionne Warwick, with Stephen Boyd as the evil 'massa'. Different look at slavery and a great performance as always, by Davis. Was released on a double bill with *Night of the Living Dead* in 1969.

18. *Dr Black and Mister Hyde*. Bernie Casey is Dr. Black, but when he takes his experimental serum, he turns into Mr. Hyde who hates pimps, prostitutes and drug dealers. Casey is awesome as he destroys all in his path.

19. *Black Mama, White Mama*. A different take on *The Defiant Ones* with Pam Grier and Margret Markov as two prisoners chained together. Markov and Grier teamed again in *The Arena*. Margret married producer Mark Damon, who she met while shooting *The Arena*, and retired. Pam is still working today.

20. *Mean Johnny Barrows*. Fred Williamson's directorial debut. He is a returning Vietnam Vet forced to work for the mob when he is unable to find a real job.

THE ENSEMBLE CAST: A GRINDHOUSE STAPLE

It may have started with *Vera Cruz* in 1954. Burt Lancaster's gang of killers was comprised of a who's who of up-and-coming actors, some who would go on to superstardom, including Charles Bronson, Ernest Borgnine, Jack Elam, Jack Lambert, John Dehner. Directed by Robert Aldrich, it was an action filled shoot 'em up and it would set the stage for things to come. In the '50s, a lot of hungry actors had used the GI Bill to study acting after serving in WWII. Most, like Borgnine, Bronson, Lee Van Cleef, Jack Palance, and others found work as heavies in the early '50s. That was about to change.

In 1960, a classic Japanese samurai epic, *The Seven Samurai*, was to be made into a western. Yul Byrnner was cast in the lead and, according to Yul, he had bought the rights from director Akira Kurosawa to make the film. He didn't. But after much wrangling and changing writers, The Mirisch Corporation would produce the film. John Sturges (*The Great Escape, Bad Day at Black Rock*) would direct. Brynner and *Wanted: Dead or Alive* TV star, Steve McQueen, were already cast; now Sturges need the rest of the seven.

Sturges tapped Charles Bronson and Brad Dexter, two actors he had worked with before. He had directed both McQueen and Bronson in *Never So Few*. He had directed Dexter in *Last Train From Gun Hill*. James Coburn was a huge fan of *The Seven Samurai* and found out about the film after his friend Robert Vaughn was cast. He auditioned and got a part. The last of the *Seven* was German actor, Horst Buchholtz, cast as a Mexican. Eli Wallach was cast without even auditioning for the part of bandit leader, Calvera. Unknowingly, Calvera would be the template for one of Wallach's best roles as Tuco, in Sergio Leone's *The Good, The Bad and the Ugly*.

There would be two major problems with production. One was the Mexican Government was not happy the way the Mexican people were portrayed in *Vera Cruz*. They had a censor on the set at all times. The Mexican peons were not allowed to get "dirty" as they had in *Vera Cruz*. Their white garments remained a pristine white, even when they were digging ditches. The Seven would get dirty. Also they changed the script as to when the villagers were supposed to go hire gun fighters; they were to just go buy guns to arm themselves. Brynner's character, Chris, suggests that it would be cheaper to hire gunfighters than buy guns. This was done so the Mexicans would not appear "weak".

The other problem was Steve McQueen. McQueen felt he should have been cast as the romantic lead, not Buchholtz. He made Buchholt's life miserable on set. In interviews with Buchholtz, Horst is almost foaming at the mouth when McQueen's name is mentioned. McQueen also got under Brynner's skin. Steve did some things in the early part of the film to draw attention to himself. He kept playing with his hat and doing things with his hands, detracting from the scene being shot. Finally Brynner told him that if he kept this up, Brynner would completely upstage him by taking off his own hat. After that, Brynner hired a crew member to spy on McQueen during his solo scenes to make sure he could top any of Steve's "business" in future sequences.

The film was given a limited release in the states, then was pulled from theaters. It was only after the film became a huge hit in Europe, was it given a wide release here to rave reviews. McQueen, Bronson, Coburn, and Vaughn became huge stars not long after. The Mirisch Corporation wanted a sequel, but at the end, only three of the Seven were still alive. They decided to bring back Byrnner and a new *Seven*.

McQueen and Buchholtz would not reprise their roles, and the producers didn't want to be chair locked by the Mexican censors again. They decided to shoot the film in Spain, where the two other sequels would be shot as well. Robert Fuller was brought in to play McQueen's character, Vin. Julian Matos would take over the role of Chico, Buchholtz's character. Warren Oates and Claude Atkins were cast, as well as Portugese actor, Virgillio Teixeira, who was well-known in Spain. Jordan Christopher rounded out the Seven. Veteran actor and legit bad ass, Emilio Fernandez (*The Wild Bunch*) was the bandit leader and his henchman was Rudolfo Acosta, who had a pedigree playing Mexican bandits and Indian renegades.

The film was released as *Return of the Seven* in 1966. The plot line was that Chico's village was raided and all the men were forced into slave labor. Chico was taken and his wife got Chris and Vin to free him and the others. Again, it was a big hit and the moviegoers wanted more. Byrnner wanted more money, so George Kennedy was cast as Chris. (Byrnner, however, would don the black outfit again in Michael Crichton's *Westworld*). This time it was *The Guns of the Magnificent Seven*, 1969. Like nine years earlier, you had a cast of hungry young actors looking to make an impact: Monte Markham, Bernie Casey, Joe Don Baker, Reni Santoni and Scott Thomas were the new guys. Veteran actor, James Whitmore rounded out the cast. Michael Ansara was the sadistic bad guy. This time the plot centered on freeing a political prisoner (Fernando Rey) from a fortress. The film was a hit, but the next one wouldn't be.

The Magnificent Seven Ride would be the weakest entry in the series. Obviously suffering from budget cuts, as one battle is fought completely off screen and a sort of weak cast of characters. An ailing Lee Van Cleef is cast as Chris, now a Sheriff. Chris is asked by a friend to help him stop a gang of bandits. Chris's wife is abducted by bank robbers and killed, as is his friend who tried to stop the gang. Tracking the bandits, he finds a town where all the men have been killed and the women raped. The gang will be coming back for the women again. Chris goes to a prison to recruit a new seven.

This time around the seven were Ed Lauter (*Deathwish 3*), James B Sikking (*Hill Street Blues*), William Lucking (*Sons of Anarchy*), Luke Askew (*Rolling Thunder*), Michael Callan, and Pedro Armendariz Jr. Unlike their predecessors, none of these guys became huge stars, but were in demand as character actors. The film seemed to rely on Van Cleef's drawing power as he was a huge star due to his spaghetti western output at the time. According to co-star Michael Callan, Van Cleef was ailing during the shoot, suffering from cancer. He was part of the cast of the John Wayne-as-Genghis Khan film, *The Conqueror*, which was filmed at the site of the atom bomb tests in Nevada. Most of the cast and crew of that film were exposed to radiation from the bomb tests, including star, John Wayne.

Part of the problem with *The Magnificent Seven* Ride was the development of the characters. In the previous films, you learned enough about each character that you cared about them. In the first *Seven*, all the characters were defined. Harry (Brad Dexter) was after a payoff, Lee (Robert Vaughn) was struggling with losing his nerve, Britt (James Coburn) was a knife-wielding perfectionist, etc. In the *Return of the Seven*, Frank (Claude Atkins) had a death wish; Colbee (Warren Oats) was a womanizer; Luis (Virgilio Teixeira) could either join the Seven or hang. In *Guns*, Chris saved Keno (Monte Markham) from a mob, Slater (Joe Don Baker) lost an arm in the Civil War; Levi (James Whitmore) was an old friend of Chris; PJ (Scott Thomas) was dying of TB; and Cassie (Bernie Casey) was a former slave. In *Ride*, the only connection between the men was that Chris had most of them put in prison. Only Skinner (Luke Askew) had a connection as he turned outlaw after being on the side of the law. Also at the climactic battle, three of the group got killed off very quickly.

The Magnificent Seven also became a TV Series and supposedly a remake is in the works.

(As an aside, while Van Cleef was playing the role that Yul Brynner had made famous, Byrnner wound up playing a role Van Cleef had made famous, *Sabata*. Byrnner was doing a spaghetti western, *Indigo Black*, which was retitled *Adios, Sabata* with much of the same cast and crew of the original *Sabata*. Van Cleef would reprise that role in *Return of Sabata*.)

The Dirty Dozen, 1967, would raise the bar for ensemble casts. Directed by Robert Aldrich and based on the book by E. M. Nathanson's novel (possibly inspired by a real life group of airborne soldiers nicknamed the "Filthy Thirteen"), *Dozen* was packed with great actors. Lee Marvin as maverick Major Reisman has to train and lead a group of prisoners behind enemy lines to take out German officers resting up at a resort. The key prisoners were Charles Bronson, Telly Savalas, Jim Brown, Clint Walker, Donald Sutherland, Trini Lopez, and a scenery chewing John Cassavetes. The army higher ups were Ernest Borgnine, Robert Ryan, George Kennedy, Ralph Meeker, Robert Webber and Richard Jaeckel.

This was an epic production. In fact it could have been in the running for an Academy Award if director Aldrich was willing to change one scene, which he wasn't. That scene was the burning of the German officers in the bunker. Aldrich refused to cut or change that scene. When Trini Lopez decided he wanted more money, he was written out and killed off-camera. Bronson, Savalas, Brown, Cassavetes, and Sutherland went on to become big stars. Cassavetes got huge props for his portrayal of Victor Franko and went on to become a groundbreaking independent director.

The floodgates of imitators, rip-offs, and revisions opened quickly. *Dirty Dozen: The Next Mission*, 1985, was a TV movie that brought back Marvin, Borgnine and Jaeckel. It wasn't even close to the original. Another lame sequel *Dirty Dozen: the Fatal Mission*, 1988, was even worse as Telly Savalas took over the role of Major Reisman. Roger Corman tried a "Dirty Half-Dozen" with *The Secret Invasion*, 1964, with Mickey Rooney, Stewart Granger, Raf Vallone, Henry Silva, Ed Byrnes, and William Campbell. Italian copycat cinema churned out a bunch of rip offs like *The Dirty Seven, The Commandos, Five from Hell*, and others. *Magnificent Seven* rip-offs included *Today We Kill, Tomorrow We Die* with Bud Spencer, Brett Halsey, and William Berger. *The Five Man Army* with Peter Graves, Bud Spenser and James Daly. Then, in a weird twist, a couple of films had the seven as bad guys. *Kill Them All and Come Back Alone* and *Seven Winchesters for a Massacre* (aka *Payment in Blood*) come to mind, wherein each of the seven killers used different weapons: knife, whip, fists, spurs etc.

Scripted by respected indie filmmaker John Sayles, *Battle Beyond the Stars*, 1980, was *The Magnificent Seven* in outer space. Seven spaceships attempt to stop John Saxon from taking over the universe. Richard Thomas, George Peppard, Sybil Danning and Robert Vaughn are part of the seven. Vaughn actually reprises his "Lee" character from the original film. The film is a lot of fun and was directed by Roger Corman. *Sweet Justice,* 1992, had a group of seven women cyclists, Kathleen Kinmont, Patricia Tallman, Marjean Holden, Michele McCormick, Cheryl Paris, and others, go after people who killed a sister of one of the group.

The king of putting together ensemble casts would have to be Sam Peckinpah. Sam worked with a lot of character actors as he wrote TV for a lot of the western series of the '50s. There was a shitload of them: *The Rilfleman, Wagon Train, The Westerner, Gunsmoke, Bonanza,* and more. Actors like Warren Oats, Jack Elam, Lee Van Cleef, Leo Gordon, LQ Jones, R.G. Armstrong, Charles Bronson, George Kennedy, and others found a lot of work doing these shows, mainly as guest heavies. Sam loved these guys. His film, *Ride the High Country,* 1962, may have been the swan song for stars Randolph Scott and Joel McCrea, but it was the start of what would become Sam's stable of stock players. Warren Oats, L.Q. Jones, Armstrong, and John Davis Chandler were Sam's guys and would continue to work with him.

As much as *Major Dundee* (1965) was an incoherent mess, these four guys starred alongside Burt Lancaster (who allegedly finished directing the film after another of Sam's benders sidelined him), Ben Johnson, Dub Taylor, James Coburn, Slim Pickens and Karl Swenson. *The Wild Bunch,* 1969, brought back Oates, Jones, Johnson, Taylor, and added Strother Martin, Ernest Borgnine, Bo Hopkins and Emilio Fernandez, who would all work for Sam again. The biggest ensemble cast by Sam was *Pat Garrett and Billy the Kid*. James Coburn and Kris Kristoferson were the leads and Sam cast just about every western character actor that was still breathing at this time: Jack Elam, Richard Jaeckel, Gene Evans, Elisha Cook, LQ Jones, RG Armstrong, Matt Clark, Chill Wills, Barry Sullivan, Jason Robards, Luke Askew, Slim Pickens, Katy Jurardo, John Beck, Emilio Fernandez, Paul Fix, Harry Dean Stanton, John Davis Chandler, Dub Taylor and Bruce Dern.

One of the lesser known, but a real ass kicker of a film was *The Immortals,* 1995. Eric Roberts masterminds a robbery with eight violent criminals. All are strangers to each other and all are dying of something. Roberts pairs each of them with another member of the gang that they hate. A homophobe is paired with a gay guy, a racist is paired with a black guy, a woman hater is paired with a woman, etc. The exceptional cast includes William Forsythe, Chris Rock, Tia Carrere, Clarence Williams III, Joe Pantoliano, and Tony Curtis. Great knock-down, drag-out, blood-splattered action.

Even some comedies had great casts. *Cannonball Run* (1981) is a collection of stars with Burt Reynolds, Dean Martin, Jack Elam, Roger Moore, Sammy Davis Jr., Peter Fonda, Farrah Fawcett and others. Ensemble casts still continue today with films like *The Expendables, Reservoir Dogs, The Devil's Rejects,* and others. These were some great films and showcased some of the best actors ever to step in front of a camera.

RED SUN: EAST-MEETS-WEST SPAGHETTI WESTERN

Charles Bronson was a busy character actor, playing mostly heavies in '50s and '60s B-westerns and crime films. Roger Corman was the first to realize that Bronson could carry a film, so Corman cast him in the lead in 1958's *Machine Gun Kelly*. Corman's Kelly was a coward with an exaggerated fear of death and dying. He is pushed deeper into a life of crime by his moll Flo, brilliantly played by Susan Cabot. Corman packed the rest of the cast with a who's who of '50s character actors. Richard Devon, Jack Lambert, Wally Campo, Frank De Kova, and Morey Amsterdam as a gay informer.

Bronson went on to be in great ensemble casts like *The Magnificent Seven, The Great Escape,* and *The Dirty Dozen*. He was contacted by Italian director, Sergio Leone, to star in *A Fistful of Dollars*. Bronson hated the script and turned it down. He was also one of many actors who turned down Leone's offer to co-star with *Eastwood in For a Few Dollars More.* Rumor also had it that he turned down the role of Tuco in *The Good, The Bad, and The Ugly*. While Bronson wasn't yet a "star" in America, he was huge overseas, especially in France. Sergio Leone was going to do an epic western, *Once Upon a Time in The West* and Bronson finally accepted one of the lead roles.

Two things worked against the film when it was released in America. Leone had always wanted to work with Henry Fonda. In fact, Fonda was his first choice to play Cornel Mortimer in *For a Few Dollars More*. Fonda was apprehensive, but Eli Wallach told him Leone was a great director and Fonda would enjoy working with him. Leone cast Fonda against type as a bad guy, and in an early scene, he kills a child. Though he also starred as the villain in Anthony Mann's popular *Firecreek* with Jimmy Stewart that same year, American audiences couldn't handle Fonda as *this* sadistic a killer.

The second thing was the film was 165 minutes long. American distributors cut out over 30 minutes, rendering the film as almost incomprehensible, and the film tanked in the States, lasting about a week. Overseas, it was a huge hit. Bronson had huge following in Europe and Asia. It was not until *Death Wish* in '74 that his career really took off in the states.

Red Sun, 1971, was an Italian/ French/Spanish co-production based a factual incident. Bronson co-starred with Japanese superstar Toshiro Mifune, who was Akira Kurosawa's lead in *The Seven Samurai, Yojimbo* and *Sanjuro*. Bronson's old friend, French heart-throb Alain Delon, was cast as the bad guy. Ursula Andress, Capucine, and spaghetti western regulars Anthony Dawson and Ricardo Palacios rounded out the cast.

Link (Bronson) and Gauche (Delon) rob a train. On the train is a Japanese Ambassador carrying an ancient Japanese sword as a gift for the President. Gauche double crosses Link, leaving him for dead. Gauche kills one of the samurai guarding the sword. Gauche takes the sword as part of the loot. The other samurai, Kuroda, is given seven days to retrieve the sword or commit ritual suicide, *hara kiri*, for failure. Gauche has now hidden the gold and has killed his men who buried it.

Link is pressed into service by the Japanese. Link tries to convince Kuroda not to kill Gauche until he tells Link where he hid the gold. Kuroda not only wants the sword, he wants Gauche dead for killing the other samurai. Link attempts to lose him, but Kuroda refuses to be put off. Link leads them to Capucine's whorehouse where Gauche's girlfriend, Christine (Ursula Andress), is waiting for him. Link hooks up Kuroda with a girl to mellow him out. Gauche send some of his men to fetch Christina, but a battle with Link and Kuroda leave all the gunmen dead except for Hyatt (Anthony Dawson).

Hyatt is told to tell Gauche that they want the gold and the sword for Christina. Hyatt tells Link that he's going to tell Gauche that he wants Link for himself. They take Christina and go looking for Gauche, but Gauche and his gang aren't the only problem. They find some of Gauche's gang dead, shot full of arrows. Seems the Comanches are raiding and killing in the area.

Christina escapes but is surrounded by Comanches. She kills one with his own knife. She is staked out in the sun with wet rawhide tied around her neck. As it dries, she slowly strangles for the amusement of the Comanches. Link and Kuroda rescues her with Kuroda battling lance and arrows with his sword. Earlier, Kuroda had stripped and was washing himself when Link stole his clothes. Kuroda, freezing, curses out Link, but agrees to not kill Gauche until he tells Link where the gold is hidden. Kuroda curses Link, calling him one son of a bitch. Link tells Kuroda that he thinks he is one hell of a man. The two now have a mutual respect for each other.

The group finds Gauche and his gang hold up in an old fort. Christina tells Gauche that link and Kuroda saved her life. Gauche asks Link what he wants. Link wants his gold and for Gauche to take a high dive in a short well. Gauche tells Link that he promised Hyatt he could kill him. Before he can act on this, Hyatt takes an arrow in the back as the Comanches attack. Gauche, realizing he is in deep shit, gives Link and Kuroda their weapons. Kuroda proves to be a one man army, wiping out Comanches with his sword and knives.

After most of Gauche's men are slaughtered, the rest leave the fort and hide in the cane breaks surrounding the fort. The Comanches set the breaks on fire. The group fights on, with Kuroda taking on the Comanche leader, lance vs. sword. Hyatt and the rest of Gauche's men are killed. Gauche mortally wounds Kuroda, thinking that Link is only after the gold. Christina tosses Gauche a rifle, but Link is faster. Gauche, wounded, taunts Link about the gold.

Link, seeing Kuroda dying, levels his gun at Gauche and says, "No, you can have it all," and shoots Gauche in the head. Link promised a dying Kuroda that he will return the sword as promised. Kuroda reminds Link he has a price on his head. Link tells him not to worry. The film ends with the sword tied to a cable were the train was going to meet Kuroda.

Red Sun was a huge hit overseas, but bombed in the states. Originally 112 minutes, US distributors cut it down to 90 minutes for the Drive-In and Grindhouse circuit. To get the PG rating, they cut out a lot of the violence and the payoff shot of full frontal nudity from Ursula Andress. *Red Sun*, however, cemented Bronson's reputation as a superstar abroad. Mifune and Bronson worked well together and had a great on screen chemistry. *Red Sun* also started a small trend of East-meets-West Spaghetti westerns.

Blood Money (1974), aka *The Stranger and the Gunfighter*, teamed Spaghetti Western icon, Lee Van Cleef with Lo Lieh, star of *Five Fingers of Death*. The two stars worked well together. *Shanghai Joe* (aka *El Mio Nome Shanghai Joe* and *My Name is Shanghai Joe,* 1973) starred Chen Lee (Myoushin Hayakawa) who was really Japanese. A virtual unknown, he moved to Italy from England in 1970, where he opened a karate academy. He was working in a laundry when he passed the screen test for *Joe*. The film features a Who's-Who of Spaghetti Western regulars including Klaus Kinski, Gordon Mitchell, and Robert Hundar. Other attempts at these films failed miserably like *Kung Fu Brothers in the Wild West* (1973) and *Return of Shanghai Joe* (1974)

Imported westerns suffered horrible cuts at the hands of US distributors. *Day of Anger* was cut from almost two hours to 95 minutes. *Red Sun* was released on VHS by Video Gems. The source print sucked. Thankfully the 112 minute version has since been released on DVD.

HE'S NOT JUST "THE OLD GUY" ON THE WALKING DEAD
SCOTT WILSON'S FIVE DECADES IN FILM

Strange thing is fame. You have been a gifted character actor for over five decades, then you get a role on one of the hottest shows ever created. Now you're a household name to millions of fans. That actor is Scott Wilson, best known today for his role as "Herschel" on the AMC zombie series, *The Walking Dead*. Obviously the modern horror fan is more concerned with now than with then. But it was back then that a skinny kid was 16th billed in the Sidney Poitier classic *In the Heat of the Night* (1967). Then another role came the same year. This one he co-starred with Robert Blake in the film adaptation of Truman Capote's seminal "fictional non-fiction" novel, *In Cold Blood*. This was the film that got Scott noticed.

In 1969 he went to Yugoslavia to be part of an ensemble cast for Sydney Pollock's surreal WWII film, *Castle Keep*. Burt Lancaster, Patrick O'Neal, Peter Falk, Tony Bill, James Patterson, and Bruce Dern were all shattered soldiers defending a castle against the German Army. Wilson is Corporal Clearboy, who falls in love with a Volkswagen. Great film filled with action and quirky characters. That same year he co-starred with Lancaster again, and Gene Hackman in *The Gypsy Moths*, directed by John Frankenheimer.

In 1971, Robert Aldrich cast him in the lead as Slim Grissom in *The Grissom Gang*. The gang were a bunch of halfwits who kidnap heiress Kim Darby. Slim is a knife-loving psychopath who falls in love with his victim. Tony Musante, Connie Stevens, Robert Lansing, and Matt Clark also appear. In 1972, Wilson would co-star and become close friends with Stacy Keach in *The New Centurions*. Based on Joseph Wambaugh's novel, both Wilson and Keach are rookie cops. George C Scott is their mentor. Erik Estrada, Clifton James, Jane Alexander and Rosalind Cash co-star. Wilson was a busy man, *Lolly-Madonna XXX* (1973), *The Great Gatsby* (1974), *The Passover Plot* (1976), and to Mexico in 1979 for *La Ilegal*. Wilson was always the fourth-billed main player in these films.

In 1980 Wilson would go back to Europe and co-star once again with Stacy Keach in what myself and others feel was his greatest role. *The Ninth Configuration* was written by *The Exorcist* author William Peter Blatty. The book was a total mindfuck, and Blatty decided he would direct the film. The cast for this film was a who's who of *the* best character actors ever assembled: Neville Brand, Richard Lynch, Moses Gunn, Jason Miller, Joe Spinell, Ed Flanders, Steve Sandor, Tom Atkins, Robert Loggia, George DiCenzo, and William Lucking. The only problem with the film was that no one saw it.

For whatever reason, prior to release the film's title was changed to *Twinkle, Twinkle Killer Kane* (the book's original title) but was marketed as a "slasher" film. Slasher films like *Friday the 13th*, *The*

Prowler, etc., were hugely popular in the '80s. The film bombed and then vanished from distribution. Prowling a used book store, I found a copy of *The Ninth Configuration*. After reading it, I really wanted to see the film. There was a theater in NYC, The 8th Street Playhouse, which ran a different movie every night at midnight. Weekends were reserved for *The Rocky Horror Picture Show*. I found out that *The Ninth Configuration* was playing.

Myself and my buddy, Rich, decided to check it out. I was drinking a six pack of Heiniken before the film started. The film was so mesmerizing and, as bad as I had to piss, I didn't want to miss a minute of this. The dialog between Keach and Wilson was fantastic. These two carried the film playing off of the on screen insanity as well as the off camera insanity.

According to actor, Tom Atkins, none of the actors had a clue what director Blatty was doing. They never knew if they were to be on the set at any given day. The film was shot in Hungary and some of the boys got into mischief. Tom Atkins told me a story about Jason Miller who had some hot blonde leading him on. They all went to some affair, but the blonde arrived with a Nigerian. Miller was fuming and proceeded to get drunk. He kept muttering about "that fuckin cunt" and what he wanted to do to her escort. Joe Spinell egged him on and Miller made a move on the Nigerian. The guy saw it coming ad moved, Miller crashed through a table and the guy started beating on him. Spinell grabbed a bottle from the bar and smashed it over the guy's head. Spinell wound up in jail for a couple of days and was pissed that hs canary froze to death while he was locked up.

Anyway with my teeth floating, I sat through the entire film. The film is a mind fuck that takes place in a castle in the Pacific Northwest. It's a lunatic asylum for servicemen. Cutshaw, Wilson's character, is an astronaut who aborted his first mission. A new Psychiatrist, Colonel Vincent Kane is brought to the castle. Kane and Cutshaw go right at it in some of the most intense interplay ever committed to film.

Kane tells his staff to let the men indulge their fantasies. This leads to Moses Gunn dressing like Superman, Miller casting *Hamlet* with an all-dog cast, and recreating *The Great Escape*. The dialog between Kane and Cutshaw is priceless. "If God existed, he's a fake, or more likely a foot. A giant all-powerful, all-knowing foot." Cutshaw proclaims. Cutshaw asks Kane that if he were to die first, would he send back a sign. Yeah, it's deep, it really is. There is also a bar fight (between Keach and professional badass Richard Lynch) to end all bar fights. The film really blew me away, and I made it to the can after the credits without pissing all over myself. A little side note, there was no part written for Joe Spinell. Spinell begged Blatty, who was a friend, to include him in the movie. Joe's part was completely adlibbed.

Wilson appeared in *The Right Stuff* in 1983, then he was back to being top billed in films like *Year of the Quiet Sun, The Aviator, Blue City, Marlowe, Young Guns II,* and other '80s films. He stayed in the '90s with a lot of fourth-billed supporting roles. He went uncredited in the horrible Stallone-driven *Judge Dredd,* 1995. He was in *G.I. Jane, Clay Pigeons, South of Heaven, West of Hell,* and several TV movies and series like *The X-Files*. The early 2000's saw him in *The Animal, Pearl Harbor, Bark, Coastlines* and *Don't Let Go*. More TV movies and TV series like *Karen Cisco* and *Law & Order*. He was mobster and father Sam Braun on *C.S.I.* Wilson was always in demand and never lacking for work.

Between 2007 and 2011 Wilson was in *The Heartbreak Kid, Big Stan, Saving Grace B. Jones, Bottle World* and a guest spot on *Justified*. In 2011, Wilson was cast in a new show, *The Walking Dead* as Hershel Greene. Fans of the show embraced Wilson's character. Some new fans thought he was something new. The character of Hershel Greene was so endearing to fans that they were really pissed when the writers killed him off.

Today, Scott Wilson has been making the rounds of the convention circuit, meeting his fans. In deciding to write this I just felt that fans might like to know just how much great work Wilson did prior to his newfound fame on *The Walking Dead*.

AWKWARD THANKSGIVING

By Rachelle Williams

I.

My career as Rachelle Williams has been many things—*awkward* is only one word I would use to describe it. So, when I saw the posting for *Awkward Thanksgiving*, I thought, "Why not? It's been an awkward holiday for me since 1999, really, so why the fuck not?"

Besides—I just wanted to work with Henrique Couto.

I needed to see what all the hype was about.

When I first met him, he had a bit part in *Demon Divas in the Lanes of Damnation*: he was wearing funny pants, had a funny beard, and laughed at funny things. He was just a funny guy. Nice enough, took no guff, and caused no problems. So, we got on well.

Flash forward a year or so, and the man is *everywhere*. Bumping into me at conventions. Smiling. Making his own movies now like he knows what the fuck is what.

And here we are in 2014. The man is a machine: tirelessly making the convention rounds, single-handedly making Facebook not suck, and *owning* Kickstarter. Couto doesn't just hit his fucking goals on a funding platform—he exceeds it. He triple Lutz'd over it, actually, with that goddamn smile on his face. Not even winded. Maybe breathing a little heavy, but that's probably just from laughing.

The best part is: that smile is genuine. The next best part: I found out what all the hype was about.

II.

2014 mostly tried to kick my ass. It succeeded only slightly. I got back up, dusted off my ass, wiggled it around a little, saw that it was still a power tush, and moved forward. What did save the year was working on *Awkward Thanksgiving*.

Adventure-seeking pal Joe Jovingo joined me for the Ohio drive from Canton to Dayton. Pal Joe was almost immediately enlisted as Production Assistant Joe. I guess I kinda knew that would happen. Hang out with me long enough and you, too, will have an IMDB.com profile, whether you like it or not. We crash-landed at Henrique's place, met his roommate Eric Widing, and blasted off to the set.

The alien invasion imagery is deliberate. Shaun and Melissa Walters allowed Henrique and his crew to take over their New Lebanon home and grounds. And I mean, hijack. All of us landed like a bunch of space invaders, *polite* but LOUD, and probably more than a little overwhelming for our kind hosts. They never let it show the entire weekend. They were warm, funny, smart, and never complained once.

Then again, if I had a house that resembled the Cordova Compound in author Marisha Pessl's *Night Film* at best, or author Mark Z. Danielewski's *House of Leaves* at worst, I would probably not complain either. Those are compliments of the highest order. Melissa cooked the meal you see in the film and allowed me to take home leftovers. Moreover, she allowed me to pet the chicks—who are now full grown chickens full of personality and spunk and I can follow their antics on Facebook. Rad folks, all around.

III.

All cast members, like the aforementioned poultry, were energetic and professional, not to mention mostly out of their artistically tortured minds. It would not be a real film set if everyone sat quietly about reading lines and meditating, however. There were no set conflicts, no diva behavior. Everyone got along. I thought for sure we'd all been mickied; however, Couto, like Richard Simmons is anti-drug. And they have to be—in order to produce the volume of work they do at the enormously high energy levels they have—they can't take fun drugs or they'd run the risk of an immediate heart attack.

And comparing Couto to Simmons is a profound moment for me. I love and respect them both for their quirks and talents—and for always remaining true to exactly who the fuck they are. As I did on this set: as Rachelle, I don't wear glasses, but the role of 'Tina' felt like it needed glasses, so I left them on. It worked. I will channel Simmons and Couto in the future if I need to reacquaint myself with my inner badass.

What also worked in the film: the pot smoking, family-bonding scene. No, it's not real pot. And yes, I accidentally tried to smoke from the wrong end. The laughter is real. Lucky for me, the snafu worked for the character. Serendipity abounded on the set.

And that serendipitous run ended when I was stationed behind my co-star during his turkey scene. I'm scarred—and you will be, too. In a good way. You don't want to go to your grave unscathed, do you? And shame on you, if you do. You need to grab life by its fat little neck and squeeze already.

IV.

The film premiered the weekend of November 8th in Dayton, Ohio, at the Englewood Cinema. I was able to attend the second premiere in Germantown, Ohio, on November 14th at the ByJo Theater. It was my first movie premiere—and the first time I would see myself on the big screen.

I had prepared well with a full dinner at The Florentine across the street and an early showing of *Big Hero 6* at the ByJo Theater to get myself ready for the 10 pm extravaganza. Like the first premiere, this one also had a hundred people in attendance—some of them not fans, friends, or shills. Some were actual strangers who wondered what they hype was all about. I could relate to that.

I can usually travel incognito. Rachelle Williams has the *She's All That* syndrome going on. Glasses off, Rachelle. Glasses on, not Rachelle. As aforementioned, I felt this role called for glasses.

And as such, after the film's end and the house lights came up—I was recognized immediately.

That was new for me. The smiles, the staring … the POINTING. All unnerving and I'm not sure how famous people do that every day. I don't think I could. But this one time was all right.

Why?

Because this film matters.

After I saw it, I realized several things:

1. Plastic surgery is a silly thing.
2. Acting can be rewarding.
3. This is the most important film I have ever done.
4. Couto nailed it. *Nailed* it. And he found the right cast to help him.

It's about my family. It's about your family. It's about us.

MAKING POLLEN

by 42nd Street Pete & Scott Brocius

Scott: Before *Pollen*, it was September when I decided to become involved with the 48 Hour Horror Film Project. The gist of it was that you are given horror genre, slasher, creature, supernatural etc., then have to write, film, score and edit it in 48 hours. A friend, Rick Bub, wanted to bring in a guy he had met at Cinema Wasteland, 42nd Street Pete. Pete was known as a Grindhouse Film Historian, whatever that was, and I quickly found out he knew a lot about older exploitation films.

Another cast member was Jenn Peters, an unknown, but eager to get involved. So we gathered at a little eatery and waited for the phone call that would give us the genre. A collective groan went up when we got "found footage". What came out of that was *Brown Zero* with myself, Pete, Jenn, Rick Bub, and a couple of others. The found footage was a commercial gone horribly wrong. It was a silly film, but it won best musical score and at its debut at the festival, people popped for it. Pete and Jenn had an on screen chemistry that worked and Brown Zero started a conversation about making an actual film.

Pete: Rick Bub had talked me into doing the 48 Hour Film Project. After we got dealt the worst hand, found footage, I showed up wearing a pimp hat, shades, a fringed jacket and a very loud tie. My "wife" was Jenn Peters. We really clicked on camera and had some fun bickering back and forth. After *Brown Zero*, Scott approached me about making a real film. He sent me a treatment, I didn't like it. I sent him something I wrote in 2006 as *A Girl's Gotta Do What a Girls Gotta Do*. It was about 3 strippers that are down & out. One rips off some tainted Extacy from a dealer she is fucking. They decided to sell it, but there are three dealers and they want their drug back. Leece, the main girl, is accidently killed by Red, one of the dealers. The drug makes her come back to life.

She wants revenge on the dealers. So she stalks and kills them in various gruesome ways. I had been hanging out with some wrestlers who really dug horror films and wanted to be in it. I had a guy getting his leg ripped off and beaten to death with it. Another guy was burned alive in a pig cooker. My character, Red, got his heart punched out. Then I had stripping, nudity and a hot lesbian scene written in. I had changed the title to the more exploitive *Blood Orgy of the Living Dead Girl*. Then forgot about it as I moved to Ohio.

Scott: Pete gave me this slasher story he had written back in 2006. I wanted to adapt it into a screenplay. The hardest part about it was nudity and lesbian orgy scenes. As awesome as they were, I knew there was no way I could get any reliable actresses to do these scenes. Also, I didn't want to do a "grind house" film as everyone is trying to do that. So I asked Pete if I could adapt it to a more character driven story and not have to rely on gore and nudity. Pete agreed to the changes. I wanted to make a film about a group of the worst humans imaginable and their personal growth or lack of it. I also wanted to keep a sense of loneliness and abandonment that permeated though out his story.

Pete: Scott had wanted to take out all the sex and gore. I had to agree, this might have worked in 2006, but after thinking about it, sex and gore has been done to death. Any no-talent so-called filmmaker can pad out their film this way. Being that there is a lot of talent involved in this film, why not let that carry the film. Jenn Peters was cast as Leece, the lead character. Although I had written the part of Red for myself, I felt I was too old to carry it off. Scott disagreed, and said the role was mine. But he wanted me to play it as 42nd Street Pete. That wasn't going to work for a lot of reasons. So I decided how I was to play Red. First, I took off my glasses.

I envisioned Red as a loser, a guy who had been dealing drugs all his life and that got him laid, that got him Leece and their love/hate relationship. It also got him in a lot of shit as he wasn't above using his own product. I played Red as a man with an undercurrent of violence, but also as a pussy who folds under pressure. Yeah, I had acted before in bits like *Batbabe: The Dark Nightie* and a couple of other films, but this was a main character. Scott cast the film using Liz, another girl who was in *Brown Zero*. Liz brought in a friend, Chelsea, to be the third girl. They brought in another friend, John to play the stooge Spike. The main drug dealer would be my buddy A. Ghastlee Ghoul from Cinema Wasteland.

In order to do this right, we had table readings once a week to get our characters down right. Scott hired some make up people and we were good to go. Now to shoot the movie in the worst cold snap this country ever experienced.

Scott: My biggest question when I started to adapt this story to a screenplay was what would cause a human to heal in a grotesque way? Yeast was my solution. As a home brewer I am very familiar with yeast and it's properties of self-replication, so I began to develop an idea I got from a brewer's magazine to use rose petals and rose hips without adding yeast. You don't have to add yeast because wild yeast collects on and around the pollen of a flower. Then I began to read about candida, which is a yeast infection of the blood. I put two of these ideas together as a possible treatment for aging and a cure for death.

Making the film was a challenge as since most of the film was shot outdoors in February in Cleveland. Then the race began filming footage for one take, having the actors run back to their cars to get warn, then resetting for another take. Batteries freezing or just running out in 15 minutes. Then concealing the crew's breath from fogging up the camera lenses, etc. Then the inside shots. This was another challenge as a majority of my cast can drink heavily if given the time and space to do so, which they did. Since we did the majority of the principle photography in 3 days, we really had to keep people from getting trashed before we could set up their scenes. In the end, I learned two lessons from making Pollen: One hide the booze before anyone gets on site, and two, never assume that 8am is too early for an actor to come to the set hammered.

Pete: I hate the fucking cold, period. It was 6 degrees out when we stopped filming Tuesday. I was heavily insulated and still cold. We shot in the Metro Park and didn't get a permit, thus paying homage to Ted V Mikels, Ed Wood and others. People were drinking heavily. I stuck to weed as I'm a tad more out of control when half-baked. No matter how well you plan stuff, shit happens. First day a camera problem set us back four hours. At times I wanted to kill Scott. But everyone took chances in the subzero weather. Scott himself ran across a semi frozen river after I beat him up. It was so cold that my switchblade would open properly.

Plans to shoot my "torture" scene in a bar were scrapped as we ran too long and we only had Ghastlee for two days. I was tortured in my own garage and it took six shots of liquor apiece to get that scene shot. That night successfully decimated my liquor cabinet. Cinema Wasteland's Ken Kish did a cameo as a Russian hit man who breaks Ghastlee's leg. We had to shoot more outside, but as luck would have it, not only did the weather remain shitty, I got sick and had to bail out for a few hours. Being that we only had the makeup people for that day, I had to suck it up and finish the scene closer to home. Yeah, when you're working with young people who party, things get a little rough, but Scott got what he wanted out of them.

Scott: So as of now, 80% of the principle photography is completed, assembly of the footage is slowly being compiled, and the story begins to unfold beyond the script. I think the hardest thing being a writer/director /editor at the same time is that you fell in love with the story you wrote and feel a little disappointed when you don't make it exactly the way it was written. So now, as the editor, I have to tell anew story and choose to hold on to what keeps the film faithful to the script and what to change to tell a compelling story. Plus when you have people like 42nd Street Pete and A. Ghastlee Ghoul, it's hard too not to let them do their own interpretation of the script and add their own twisted twists.

Pete: There is still some footage that needs to be shot. When doing an indie film, you have to adapt. There was a lot of adapting on this one. Did Ghastlee and I play with it? Sure, that's why I felt Bob would be a good addition as we worked together a lot and can play off of each other. Every film has a breakout performer, as does *Pollen*. If anyone 'owns' this film, its Jenn Peters. I have never seen anyone adapt to a role like she did and take over the film. She has the magical 'it" I saw it in *Brown Zero* and I saw it in *Pollen*. It's her turn. For a first time actress she steals every scene she is in and makes it hers. If she chooses to continue acting, I really feel she has the ability to be great. She was pleasure to work with as was everyone involved.

So what will *Pollen* be? Not what I envisioned, probably not what Scott envisioned. As a writer, you can do a lot with words, but sometimes the words don't translate into a good film. *Pollen*, however, will be a good film. Right now it's a puzzle that needs to be put together. Trick to that is, treat it like a baby, nurture it, let it grow and, above all, don't rush it. Now by letting people in on some of the details, I would hope it gets them curious enough to want to see it. Will we do another film? I'd say yeah, but let's learn from this one. Everything is a learning experience and when making a film, you have to figure out what hat fits you. You can't do it all, you have be a team player. We have a great team that has the potential to do great things. So I say let's do it.

THE MIDNIGHT MOVIE

Someone figured out in the early '70s that people were hanging out at night later than ever. Bars in NYC closed at 4am, so between say 11pm to 4am, night owls looked for a diversion. Enter the Midnight Movie. There was a film, *El Topo,* 1970, that defied description. Some called it a Spaghetti Western from Hell. It was a mindfuck, plain and simple, especially for stoners. Violence, gore, sex, real deformed people, nudity, yeah, it held its audience, but where to find that audience? Why right down the ass end of 8th avenue.

There was a theater, The Elgin, in close proximity to West Village, it catered to a "hippie" crowd. One night, they ran a mystery film at midnight, the one and only *El Topo.* It blew the collective minds of the stoned out audience. Word of mouth drew in SRO crowds on Friday and Saturday night. Andy Warhol showed up, then it became the hip film to see. John Lennon and Yoko liked it so much that they had someone buy the rights and release it to the mainstream. It tanked as it only worked with a certain crowd. And that crowd wasn't the Saturday night date crowd. I was dragged to see it as we thought it was a Spaghetti Western, something that I was really into. When you expect one thing and get another it alters your perception. I was 20-years-old and when my mind was set on one thing, I didn't want something else. Add to that the amount hooch and smoke in my system, well, I don't have to draw you a picture do I?

The Elgin needed another draw for Midnite crowd. Why not put in a '30s scare film called *Reefer Madness*? Theater full of pot heads, film about pot, duhhh, yeah, and it worked. But you had to alternate as *Madness* was a short film and *El Topo* ran almost 2 hours. So why not team it with another '30s film that had been banned. *Freaks* was made by Tod Browning right after *Dracula.* He was told to make a film more horrifying than *Frankenstein. Freaks* was that film. It was banned in Britain for over 30 years and basically ended Browning's career. It wound up on the road show circuit under titles like *Nature's Mistakes* and *Forbidden Love.* It found a new home at The Midnite Show.

George Romero's *Night of the Living Dead* was released in 1968. It came back in 1969 on the bottom half of a double bill with *Slaves*. Then it went to the Kiddee Matinee. The Kiddee Matinee was basically a couple of Warner Brothers Cartoons, a Three Stooges short, and two black and white horror films. *Night of the Living Dead* was dumped into the mix. It was a disaster. Some kids actually went into shock. That was the end of the Kiddee Matinee. *Night of the Living Dead* was tailor-made for the Midnite Show and drew huge crowds. The Elgin was now not the only place running Midnite shows. Other theater owners and chains took notice of this phenomenon and saw dollar signs.

In 1977 came the ultimate Midnight Movie, one that would break attendance records and have a longevity way beyond its initial flop release in 1975. That film was *The Rocky Horror Picture Show*. Tim Curry was the "sweet transvestite from Transsexual, Translyvania" Dr Frank N. Furter, Richard O'Brien, Susan Sarandon, Barry Bostwick, and Meatloaf rounded out the cast. It was a musical and upon hitting the Midnite circuit, inspired audience participation. Fans showed up dressed as the film's characters. During the wedding, they threw rice and other objects at different times. Released by 20th Century Fox and basically dumped after failing to attract the "straight" audiences, its renewed life at rep theaters like the 8th Street and Waverly where it ran every Friday and Saturday night, mainstream theaters wanted in on this. And they got it. *Rocky Horror* Midnight Shows sprang up all over the country. The film ran for over a decade in some venues. News crews would set up before the shows, interviewing the costumed fans. If you were to crown a King of the Midnight Movies, or maybe Queen, *Rocky Horror Picture Show* was it.

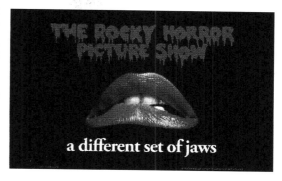

Many theaters started Midnite Shows, but sometimes their choices of films weren't the greatest. During a screening of *Mr. Mike's Mondo Video* at The Totowa Cinema in NJ, drunken fans rioted because the film was so bad. Cinema 46 in West Paterson was the only theater that would show unrated films like *Dawn of the Dead, Texas Chainsaw Massacre 2*, etc. They ran the longer version of *Dawn of the Dead* for a midnight show. Multiplexs wanted in, but didn't seem to "get it". Some would run *Rocky Horror*, others were loath to clean up the mess made by the patrons, so they ran "concert" films. *Jimi Hendrix Rainbow Bridge, Led Zepplin's The Song Remains the Same,* and others. My friends were really into the concert films; I wasn't. I was drinking heavily back then so by midnight I was almost comatose. Film would start, I'd start snoring. This pissed off the guys and people close by. I didn't give a fuck as I was tanked.

Some theaters tried to create their own Midnite Shows by finding films they felt would draw. *The Cars That Eat People* from Australia couldn't even draw flies. People walked out as no cars really ate people. Charles Band created another "classic" that bombed out big time, *The Best of Sex and Violence*. Narrated by John Carradine, it was a trailer collection. This was the General Cinema's chains Midnight Movie. It ran only once. The Capitol Theater in beautiful Passaic, NJ, was a porn grinder by day, a concert venue by night and had one of the weirdest Midnite Shows ever presented. The place was a dilapidated Grindhouse in a dangerous, high crime area. During their daily porn showings, they would have overage strippers performing between films. It was comical as patrons would sit far away from each other during the films, then all rush the stage for good seats when the strippers came on.

The Capitol's Midnight Show wasn't just a movie; it was a collection of film and TV bloopers, 3 Stooges shorts, and all kinds of weird stuff in between. It ran until 4 am. Back then, we would spend Saturday cruising around smoking weed and listening to music. By Midnight we were looking for something to do, so we went to The Capitol. After settling in, we sent one guy, Gasoline, to get us something to drink. He was gone for about 20 minutes, then came running down the aisle with two cases of beer. "How the fuck did you get this in?" someone asked. Gasoline said when he went to the snack bar, they told him the fountain was broken and he should go across the street and get something. Two cases of beer is what he got. We proceeded to get hammered. You could smoke in theaters back then, so many joints were consumed during the film.

The bloopers and out takes were classic, you had a *Star Trek* reel, you had screw ups from *Gun Smoke, Have Gun, Will Travel, Abbott and Costello Meet Frankenstein*, plus crazy commercials, and just weird clips. About 3 am they put on this really fucked up '30s film about Captain Carswell, some kind of deep Sea Explorer. They would show stock footage of sharks, octopus, whales, etc. Then our intrepid Captain would drop trou and jump into the sea to do battle. When this turd ended at 4 am, there was dead silence until someone muttered loudly, "That guy is a jerk off". Night over, I tried to get up, but my legs fell asleep. We all carried each other out. Good times!

In 1982 Frank Henenlotter created the last great Midnight Movie, *Basket Case*. Frank filmed *Basket Case* on and around 42nd Street. Frank is a huge film buff and, like myself, spent quite a bit of time in those Grindhouses. *Basket Case* found a home for quite a few years at The Waverly Theater in the Village. The place was packed for *Basket Case* and *The Rocky Horror Show* every weekend. To celebrate its first year there, Big Macs were handed out. Big Macs were what Belial, the creature in the basket, ate. Theaters declined in the late '80s as the home video market was keeping people, well, home. By then the Elgin was long gone. The 8th Street Playhouse, which had a different Midnight Show every day, also folded. With the plethora of weird, dangerous drugs that the '80s spawned, crowds got rowdier and that led to the end of the Midnight Show. Plus realtors, with the help of politicians, were squeezing the remaining free standing theaters out of business.

Some tried to hold on, a few, like Variety Photoplays on the East Side, switched to porn. But that was short lived as health inspectors, using the AIDS crisis as a reason, wrote up violations that closed down most of these places. There was, however, still a market for Midnight. In 2008 Wildeye Releasing was working with The Pioneer Two Boots Theater, one of the few free-standing theaters left. They were running double bills and contacted me to come in. They showed great stuff like *Zombie, The Corpse Grinders, Blood Sucking Freaks* and more. We teamed up to bring porn back to the big screen after 25 years with the John Holmes film, *Dear Pam,* and had porn legend, Jamie Gillis, come in as a guest. We started getting SRO crowds, then the axe fell. The owner of the building raised the rent to 25K a month. It was over. Our last show was on Halloween Night as we ran *Night of the Living Dead* to a packed house. We hung out until sunrise in the lobby, commiserating about the end of an era.

NOTHING TO SEE HERE!
By Bill Adcock

Horror fans, I've noticed, never shut the fuck up about Italian horror. I hear endless droning about "Lucio Fulci this," and "giallo that" and "Dario Argento blah blah blah..." trailing off into a grunting, sweaty stroke-fest. Everyone's got such a raging hard-on for Italian horror that I think a lot of horror fans tend to forget other countries exist with their own horror film traditions. Oh, sure, J-Horror and K-Horror got their respective days in the sun, and every once in a while you'll get someone who can talk about Ozsploitation, but I find more and more that if I mention some of my favorite international horror films I'm met with blank stares and "huh...never heard of it..."

I fucking love Spanish Horror, and I'm ready to teach you to love it too.

First lesson is Amando de Ossorio, and his quartet of "bloodthirsty undead" movies known collectively as *The Blind Dead* series. While Italy was content to recapitulate Romero over and over again with more and more marinara drizzled over the zombies each time, de Ossorio created his own brand of walking dead, with their own back story, motivations, and methods of stripping and killing hotter-than-hell Spanish ladies. For the purposes of this article, I'm just going to cover the first two films in the series, *Tombs of The Blind Dead* and *Return of the Evil Dead* because I've got a lot to say about both of them. All references hereafter are to the Blue Underground DVD releases of these films, which have really crisp, perfectly restored prints with all the eurosleaze intact.

Tombs of the Blind Dead opens with Virginia and her boyfriend on vacation, when they run into Betty, Virginia's old lesbian lover from back at school. When boyfriend and Betty start making eyes at each other, Virginia grabs her suitcase and jumps off the train, walking in the direction of the haunted ruins of the monastery of Berzano. She sets up camp and strips down, baring her luxuriously round and tan-lined rump for the audience in the process, but as soon as night falls an army of withered, leather-skinned knights drag themselves out of the grave, swords in hand, and begin to stalk her through the ruins. She tries to hide, but the eyeless revenants find her anyways—the panicked beating of her heart gives her away to their supernaturally sharp ears. The knights run her to ground and surround her, sinking their teeth into her flesh (well, who wouldn't?) and drinking her blood.

These are the Knights Templar—a crusading order of holy warriors corrupted by the influence of satanic powers in the East, who became necromancers and virgin-blood-drinkers upon returning home to Europe. According to *Tombs*, when the Templars were finally tracked down and executed they were hung from trees and left for the crows to eat their eyes, hence their current blindness.

The rest of the film follows Betty and boyfriend as they try to find Virginia—along the way, they fall in with a gang of smugglers, Betty gets raped, and the Templars, now awoken and hungry, set their sightless gaze and ravenous hunger on the modern day.

Tombs is a fantastic film, and a lot of that can be laid right at the feet of the Templars—they're an amazing creation, and I think the last truly original cinematic undead. They're not quite vampires, or mummies, or zombies, but mixing and matching elements of all three, and it works out well; watching the film, you feel like they absolutely could be a creation of medieval folklore instead of 1970s Eurosleaze.

But it's not just the Templars; the writing and cinematography are beautiful here. Unlike a lot of Italian horror, it's not just a string of lush dreamy visuals held together by the threadbare vagaries of a plot, there's actually a really solidly written script here with logical progression of events and believable characters—it's a good movie, beyond the zombies and bouncing butt-cheeks.

I focus on Virginia's story above even though it covers only maybe a third of the film, but it's definitely my favorite part of the film. It reminds me of *Psycho* in the way it sets up this woman to be our focal point character and gets us emotionally invested in her just in time to kill her off and set the real plot in motion; this sequence also showcases what a wizard de Ossorio was when it came to utilizing his sets (a real ruined medieval monastery, which just goes to show, shoot in Europe. Gothic sets are way cheaper). When Virginia is exploring the monastery in daylight, the ruins seem very open and airy; once night falls, they become claustrophobic, a nightmare labyrinth that the Templars can navigate, but you can't.

With *Tombs of the Blind Dead* being such an excellent film, it comes as no surprise that its immediate sequel, *Return of the Evil Dead*, aka *Return of the Blind Dead*, aka *Attack of the Blind Dead* isn't quite as good as its predecessor. However, a step down from excellent is still damn good, and *Return* suffers the most in originality, rather than overall quality.

Return revises the Templars' origin story, expanding the monastery of Berzano into the village of Bouzano, and showing the 14th-century peasants of Bouzano cornering the Templars one by one and burning out their eyes, instead of leaving them for the crows to eat. Five hundred years later (which doesn't quite work...if the Templars were killed off in the 1300s, how is the 500th anniversary in 1973?) the village of Bouzano is celebrating the anniversary of killing the Templars, and with the amount of whiskey he's trucked in, the openly-corrupt mayor is looking to ride this party all the way to reelection.

Unfortunately, the guy the mayor hired to handle fireworks used to be an item with the hot piece of ass secretary the Mayor's been trying to squeeze up on, and seeing them rekindle their old relationship sets the Mayor on a path to having the guy quietly shot. Unfortunately for this plan, the village hunchback decides this is a great opportunity to sacrifice a virgin and resurrect the Templars!

Return starts strong enough with a great sequence involving a Templar getting a face full of torch, and the final act is one of the tautest thriller sequences I've ever seen as our heroes try to hold their breath and sneak past the Blind Dead, but in between...There's things I like. Don't get me wrong. like the efforts to alert the authorities to the return of the Templars, and I really like the irony as each link in the hierarchy tries to alert their superiors, only to be given the same runaround and dismissal they gave to the guys under them until it was too late.

But for the most part, the middle of the film feels like another tired retread of *Night of the Living Dead*: a confined location, barricaded against the hordes of undead milling around outside, occupied by people who are too busy bickering to survive. And that's a disappointment, for me at least. If I wanted to watch someone do *Night*, I'd just watch *Night*, and after the creativity and imagination shown with *Tombs*, it's a real let-down to see Ossorio turn to such threadbare material with *Return*.

Overall, however, I think *Return* is for the most part a decent follow up to *Tombs*, and certainly worth watching, especially if you like horror movies that have the balls to not only put small children in immediate visceral danger, but keep them there for ten minutes, and have the skill to maintain that sense of tension all the way through. In short? Watch *Tombs of the Blind Dead* and *Return of the Evil Dead*. Get the Blue Underground editions (you'll find no better) and watch the riginal Spanish language version. Yes, that means reading subtitles. Man up and do it. You and your horror nerd cred will thank me for it.

FUORILEGGE NELLO SPAZIO:
THE GIRLS OF *42ND STREET* & *FORCED ENTRY* (1973)
TWO FILMS THAT EPITOMIZE NYC IN THE '70s

Andy Milligan may have been one of the worst filmmakers ever, but even he could get something right. Andy lived in the shittiest section of Times Square. He lived and breathed "the Deuce", and being that he was part of that whole sexual underground that permeated the area, who better than to make a film about bottom feeding whores, drag queens and hustlers? I had started hanging out on "The Deuce" about 1968. The conversations and scenarios depicted in this film I had heard or witnessed firsthand. My fondness for alcoholic beverages took me to several of the areas dive bars, bars that were inhabited by all sorts of human flotsam.

These were filthy, predatory people, looking for their next hustle. It was all about tricking and sometimes being tricked. Even the most streetwise hooker could pick up the wrong trick. She might wind up with a beating, a slashing or even murdered. Another dead hooker wouldn't get much attention from the police as in that time period, murders were common place. Low end pimps would hang out in bars like Topps, on the worst corner of the "Deuce". Or directly across from Port Authority Bus Terminal, The Terminal Bar, home of the ugliest $5 whores in NYC. Even the fuckin' bowling alley bar, right inside Port Authority, had hookers and pimps working out of it.

Heroin was epidemic then. It wasn't unusual to have a junkie couple trying to hustle up money for their next fix. The guy would come into a bar as approach patrons about his hot girlfriend giving blowjobs for $10. If you were stupid enough to take the bait, one of two things would happen. You would either be robbed the minute you entered the room, or the girl would be comatose and couldn't perform. Either way, you were out $10 and maybe your wallet, watch, and jewelry. "The Deuce" was loaded with rip-off artists. They promised everything from drugs and girls to hot color televisions. Weed and coke usually turned out to be oregano and baking powder. Loose joints were sold, but would you buy a joint licked closed by a junkie with festering sores on his lips? Not this guy. I had good connections.

"Getting a girl" was classic scam usually run by black guys. They would see a group of marks, usually high school or college kids. He would strike up a conversation and it would drift around to "You want girls, I got me some real honies." He would tell them. He would collect $10 each, they give them an address. They would be told to wait 10 minutes for him to "set things up". When the guys went to the address they would find an empty room, or a room with someone living there oblivious to the scam. The other scam was to have the girl entice a guy to a room, then some black dude would barge in screaming, "What are you doing with my wife?" Of course the trick would be naked by then and easy to take from. Many a dumb white boy took a bus back to Jersey with a deflated ego, a hard on, and no wallet.

Milligan knew the ins and outs of the game, after all, he lived there. Having been ripped off by every distributor he dealt with, he would come back to William Mishkin, even though he despised him, it was better than nothing. Mishkin made and released films aimed at the motley Times Square crowd. Along with Milligan's sexploitation and horror films, Miskin released a lot of other films including the riot inducing *Fight for Your Life*. Mishkin knew that *Girls of 42nd Street* would appeal to 42nd Street audiences. It was a sleazy slice of life that they could relate to. So Mishkin changed the title to the more lurid *Fleshpot on 42nd Street* and created one sheets and print ads that would lure in patrons.

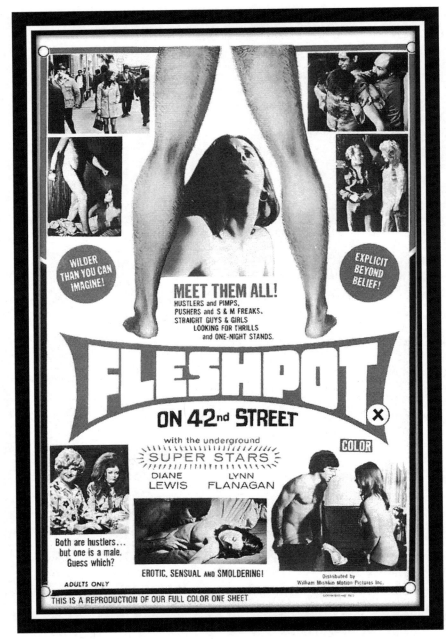

Laura Cannon, billed as "Diane Lewis", is Dusty, a low rent hooker who came to NYC looking to be a model and failed. She took to hooking rather than go 9 to 5. She is a thief, robbing one trick, then fencing the goods, tricking with the fence and robbing him too. She meets up with her drag queen cohort Cherry (Neil Flanagan). Cherry is frightening: a man with a dress and a wig, who throws Dusty tricks he either doesn't want or can't handle. Dusty does the same to Cherry, giving her a trucker who beats the shit out of her when he discovers a trouser snake. In Milligan's world, it's all about hustling or being hustled. Dusty gets a trick named Jimmy who has her "service" a card game that turns into a brutal gang bang. One of the bangers is future *Last House on the Left* star and future XXX director, Fred Lincoln.

When Dusty, Cherry, and others gather to commiserate at a bar, the conversations are as real as anything I had overheard or was drawn into at one of these dives. The dialogue is overlapping and, at times, incomprehensible, but it sort of adds to the sleazy ambiance of the film. At a 42nd Street bar, Dusty meets Bob Walters (Harry Reems), a nice guy with a good job. Bob doesn't hold Dusty's job against her. He's comfortable with her and love blooms. But in Milligan's world tragedy will strike. Bob lives in Staten Island. When Dusty walks with him to the Staten Island Ferry, Bob is hit by a car and killed. The film ends with Dusty picking up another trick on The Deuce and you get the impression that she will soon join the ranks of hookers that have died from a drug overdose.

To me, *Fleshpot* is an incredible piece of film that captures the true ambiance of the early '70s pay-for-sex hustle scene. Yeah, the films has flaws, the main one being Milligan. Obviously shooting from a car driving down 42nd street, he fails to capture any of the marquees that lit up The Deuce. Laura Cannon had done about twenty-three sex films prior to *Fleshpot*. She was also the first hardcore porn star to appear in Playboy Magazine. She worked with Reems again in Shaun Costello's brutal *Forced Entry*. Reems played a deranged raping and murdering Vietnam vet and was chilling in this role. Laura was actually his real life girlfriend for a while but she just vanished after making *Teenage Nurses* in 1974.

Andy Milligan kept on churning out grade- Z horror films. He was better at sexploitation with films *like Gutter Trash, Tricks of the Trade, Depraved, The Filthy Five* and others. His last film, *Surgikill*, was in 1989. Milligan died of AIDS in 1991. He was 62.

William Mishkin lived to be 88 and died in 1997. His son, Lew, had taken over the company and drove it into the ground. Lew hated exploitation films and really hated Andy. He destroyed any and all promotional material for these films, and had the prints melted down for their silver nitrate content. These films are lost forever. Lew died at age 60 from a brain tumor. Those in the know had said that if Andy had been still alive, he would have pissed on Lew's grave.

The Girls of 42nd Street has never been given a decent release outside of a Something Weird Video VHS. Subsequent releases have been so grainy that they are unwatchable or are completely missing the opening credits. This is a film that begs to be rediscovered, but sadly, I don't think any of the original elements remain, but hope springs eternal.

Forced Entry was an entirely different animal. The film just oozes sleaze and grime from every pore. It captures the filthy ambiance that was NYC in the early '70s. Created by former loop performer, Shaun Costello (under one of his many aliases, Helmuth Richler), he wrote, directed, edited and did the make-up effects. The film was shot in '71, but no one would release it. Chelly Wilson's distribution arm, Variety Films, released the film in '74. The film was a hardcore mindfuck. Naturally it made the rounds of her Avon chain of theaters.

Hanging out with a few guys, we were walking past The Eros I, before it became The Venus. Half lit up, we decided to see what looked like a "roughie". The film was a libido stomper. It went beyond your usual roughie into brutal murder. The guys I was with couldn't handle it, so we left midpoint into the film. I was 21 and more interested in scoring real pussy (as opposed to celluloid pussy). So I spent more time picking up hookers than watching porn. Considering I was peddling 8mm films since I was 17, there wasn't too much I hadn't seen.

But the scuzzy ambiance of the film stuck with me. I noticed it bounced all around the Times Square porn grinders into the '80s. Then came The Meese Commission under half dead president, Ronald Reagan. Avon Films were singled out as "the most vile and violent examples of mob controlled pornography." *Forced* and other Avon films were quickly yanked off of video store shelves. Prints disappeared from the porn grinders as well. I had almost forgotten about the film until I found a bootleg VHS at NYC Liquidators.

The tape was a grainy 5th generation piece of crap, but I watched it anyway. It was a porn/horror hybrid, the first of its kind. Costello incorporated real footage of the Vietnam War, thus creating the sub-genre of "deranged Vietnam Vet on a rampage." The film looked like you would have to sand blast it to clean it up. NYC was a grim, nasty place in the '70s. Crime and drug use was rampant, the city was on the verge of bankruptcy, and a strike had garbage piled on the streets six feet high. The Big Apple was rotten to its core.

Years later, I'm looking at stuff on EBay when I see a print of *Forced Entry* up for bid. Then I see that Mike Raso from Alternative Cinema was the high bidder. Having a gentleman's agreement not to butt heads on EBay, I called Mike and told him that he had to get this film, no matter what the cost, and that I would put up $$ if needed. He won the film, but then things got weird. Alternative was thrilled about getting the film. They had me write some liner notes and do an on-camera intro. All that went to shit when they contacted Costello and *he* agreed to do notes and stuff, but he could be the only one. So, without me knowing it, my stuff was dropped.

Stranger yet was that Art Ettinger asked me to write about *Forced Entry* for Ultraviolent Magazine. I had contacted Bill Landis, of The Sleazoid Express, for a few comments. He gave me some comments, some of it really vile stuff concerning Jamie Gillis, who wasn't even in the film. Then again, without my knowledge, Landis pulled his comments from the magazine. After a while, I learned that a lot of things Landis said and wrote were total bullshit. Landis seemed to have nothing good to say about anyone, even people who gave him work. People like Joel Reed, Carter Stevens, Gillis and others were baffled at the venom Landis spewed at them. Bottom line was Landis was a junkie and junkies are delusional wastes of humanity as nothing is ever their fault.

Forced Entry featured an over-the-top performance by Herb Streicher, credited here as "Tim Long".

Streicher achieved lasting fame as "Harry Reems". But he's not the goofball that we had seen in many porn films. In *Forced*, he is a shattered Vietnam vet working as a gas station attendant. He gets the addresses of woman patrons from their credit cards. Then he follows them home, rapes and kills them. *Forced* opened with flashing police lights and a crime scene. There was a body with a massive head wound. Then we get into the story. The tagline on the print ads and poster read "He was taught to Kill—Rape Was His Own Idea".

Reems walking though Times Square sees the crowds turn into villagers and men turn into soldiers. When the atrocity footage runs, Reems gets a deranged look on his face and goes hunting. Fear fuels the character as he gets off on his victims begging for mercy. He follows a woman, Laura Cannon, back to her apartment. He drags her out of the shower and holds a gun to her head. "Suck my prick!" he screams at her. "Stop for one minute and I'll pull the trigger." He has a deranged look on his face as he ass rapes her in as scene that's hard to watch. Some of the most hate-filled diatribes ever committed to film fly out of his mouth. "Tell me it hurts!" he yells at her. "Starting to bleed, are ya? You don't know what bleeding is! I'm gonna show you a lot of bleeding." He keeps saying this over and over. "You're no better than the gooks in 'Nam!" he screams. He climaxes with a flurry of explosions and gunshots in his mind as more atrocity footage of dead Vietnamese children flashes across the screen. "I didn't like that," he screams at her. "You got shit on my prick!" He slices her up brutally and kisses her as she dies. The whole thing is a libido killer and hard to watch.

His next victims are two stoned-out hippie chicks. He follows them back to their place and breaks in on them. The two are so fucked up that they laugh at him. This confuses him. They start talking dirty and coming on to him. "Don't touch me!" he yells. More war footage goes through his mind. "Stay away from me!" he yells as he falls to the floor. Images of his victims run though his mind as the girls grope him.. His insanity overtakes him and he puts the gun to his head, then pulls the trigger. Fear, his weapon, has been turned against him. Reems was so convincing in this role, and got a lot of heat for it, that he refused to play another psycho character. Costello single-handedly created this genre which led to other "Vietnam vet on a rampage" films like *Rolling Thunder, Rambo, Poor White Trash 2*, and others. Buddy Giovinazzo's *Combat Shock* used Vietnam Newsreel footage as did several other films.

Forced Entry was a ground breaking exploitation film. It mirrors the uglier side of the '70s. You might not agree with the subject matter, and the sex scenes are ugly and hate filled, so much so that they are a turn off. But then the '70s were a transition period for every type of film. Film makers weren't bound by studios as they are today. They took chances, took risks and that is why so many great films came out of that era. Forced Entry was only available from some shady video companies using the Avon tape as a master. When I saw that print on Ebay, I knew it would be something fans would really want to see. I don't know what the fate of other prints of Forced Entry was. They may have been destroyed or are in the hands of private collectors. Thankfully Alternative Cinema put a lot of effort in restoring and

releasing this formerly "lost" film.

LUIGI COZZI'S STAR CRASH
By Robert Morgan

Skintight vinyl outfits, cheap special effects, outrageous violence, campy dialogue, and acting hammy enough to give the average viewer high blood cholesterol...if you have never seen Luigi Cozzi's insanely inspired, fast-paced outer space adventure *Star Crash* then prepare thyself for a tale as old as space and as lurid and colorful as a 1950's EC Comics sci-fi title (with the subtlety to match).

It's very easy for me to determine what exactly constitutes a bad movie. The worst crime a movie can commit in my eyes is to offer nothing of value to the audience. It can be violent, vulgar, and downright morally reprehensible as long as the proper elements for creating an entertaining feature are there and being put to good use. Even when a movie is made with little in the way of money or resources if it has plenty of enthusiasm and energy it can leap the largest gaps in logic in a single bound. Such is the case with *Star Crash*. It's just an all-around great time at the movies.

Filmed under the alternate title *The Adventures of Stella Star*, Cozzi's attempt to cash in on the *global Star Wars* phenomenon was made under conditions that would have driven the perennially dissatisfied perfectionist George Lucas to suicide. Until early 2011 I knew of *Star Crash* only by reputation. Throughout my youth I saw the dazzling Charter Entertainment VHS box art at my local video store repeatedly during my frequent quests for choice weekend rentals, but I was never seized by the urge to give it a shot. To me it looked stupid beyond words, and I had no idea who any of the actors were. Except for David Hasselhoff. But my love for the Hoff had faded considerably in the years since the cancellation of *Knight Rider*, so fuck that guy.

As you can already tell, I was a bit of a judgmental prick as a kid.

When Shout! Factory gave *Star Crash* its first official DVD release in the final months of 2010 as part of their short-lived "Roger Corman's Cult Classics" line I knew the time was right to finally indulge in Cozzi's underrated labor of love. First of all, I found it oddly intriguing that the DVD was a two-disc affair that promised an indulgence of bonus features as well as the finest video and audio presentation of the movie since it first played theaters in the U.S. as a release through Corman's New World Pictures in the late 70's.

Second of all, I knew before the DVD was announced that Stephen Romano, author of the beautiful alternate universe exploitation cinema tribute *Shock Festival*, was contributing heavily to the extras due to the fact that he was possibly the greatest *Star Crash* fan in the known universe. Even if I ended up hating the movie the supplements would be at least one watch before the DVD went into the pile of flicks I would be soon trading it for store credit at the neighborhood MovieStop.

Finally, I had seen the original trailer—the last Joe Dante assembled as New World's trailer editing king before pursuing his own celluloid dreams—on the first volume of Synapse Films' *42nd Street Forever* series over five years earlier. Hard to believe it now but there was a time when the intention of a trailer was to excite audiences and guarantee the presence of their asses in seats without the need to give every single memorable moment in the movie away in advance. You baited them, hooked them, and then reeled the suckers in, but at least you gave them bait tantalizing enough to get them on the hook.

Since the plot of *Star Crash* was all over the goddamned map Dante didn't have the luxury of compacting it into a tight two minutes. So he did the next best thing and created a montage of the movie's eye-popping, brain-melting action and effects. It was colorful, energized like a fifth grader on a Pixy Stix bender, and played like the greatest amateur short film ever made by an enthusiastic film school student who grew up with fond memories of watching *It! The Terror from Beyond Space* or *The Angry Red Planet* on Saturday afternoons.

I had a feeling I would enjoy *Star Crash*, but never in my wildest dreams would I ultimately find it to be an infinitely more entertaining movie than the original Star Wars. That all changed after my first viewing, and my second, and my third, and so on. Cozzi had my attention from the opening shot: a spaceship drifts dreamily past the camera as such a close distance even a blind man could tell it was a plastic miniature, and at the very end the name "Murray Leinster" can be seen emblazoned on the hull. If you think that's an odd name to give to a massive intergalactic vessel then you're not at the level of science fiction geekery as our fearless director Luigi.

Murray Leinster, born William Fitzgerald Jenkins, was one of the most prolific writers of sci-fi in American history. In his lifetime he wrote hundreds of short stories and novels and countless scripts for film and television under a variety of pseudonyms. His name may not have commanded the same immediate attention and respect granted to his peers in the genre like Ray Bradbury, Isaac Asimov, and Harlan Ellison, but Leinster spent his life doing what he loved and entertaining his readers with fantastic tales of worlds never known and sights that will likely never exist.

By putting the name of Murray Leinster, who passed away at the age of 78 only a few years before *Star Crash* went into production, on the first spaceship glimpsed in his movie Cozzi was simultaneously paying tribute to one of his heroes and signaling to the members of the audience who understood the reference that as long as they came to have the best time imaginable he was going to do his best to not let them down. That name was the director's mission statement, and as far as I'm concerned Luigi Cozzi didn't fail.

The director's love of sci-fi and fantasy infuses every frame of *Star Crash* as if he was administering a life-saving pharmaceutical cocktail to a dying person. It's what really defines this movie and prevents it from being classified as what many have labeled it over the years, a lame Italian rip-off *Star Wars*. People tend to forget that the original (if you can call it that) *Star Wars* was itself a big-budget mix tape of the films and filmmakers that influenced its creator. Lucas took several genres that were practically moribund at the American box office—not just sci-fi but also westerns and samurai epics - and fused them together. Both Lucas and Cozzi owe a great debt to the classic space adventure comics of decades past, but only Cozzi chooses not to shy away from acknowledging their invaluable influence on his work.

The plot is pure, Grade A, top-of-the-motherfuckin'-line pulp and once it takes off it rarely pauses for a breath. Cozzi piles on the characters and action but never lets them overwhelm each other and maintains a brisk pace for each of *Star Crash*'s 91 minutes (if you're watching the U.S. cut released by New World—Cozzi's preferred cut runs five minutes longer). In the opening sequence the crew of a spaceship on a secret mission at the behest of the Emperor of the Known Universe (future Oscar honoree Christopher Plummer) is overcome by mysterious forces represented by a dollar bin spectacle of blood red lighting and magnified globules of lava lamp matter. Where it comes from we will soon know.

First things first, Cozzi treats us to a credits sequence that plays over a swooning soundtrack composed in a matter of weeks by the legendary John Barry. That's right friends, the man who gave musical voice to James Bond was selected (after Ennio Morricone proved unavailable, or unwilling, for the job) to enliven Cozzi's zippy galactic thrill ride with a lush, glorious orchestral score that plays like the swingin' 60's tiki lounge remix of John Williams' *Star Wars* themes. The main title piece alone is one of the most beautiful works Barry ever composed, but the entire soundtrack overflows with mystery, elegance, and a refreshing playfulness that reminds us that it's okay not to take *Star Crash* too seriously. It's a gem of a score and one of my favorites.

After the credits we meet our heroes, Stella Star (Caroline Munro, *Maniac*) and her faithful companion Akton (*Marjoe Gortner, Bobbie Joe and the Outlaw*), as they're being pursued by the space police lead by the stern police chief Thor (Robert Tessier, *The Longest Yard*) and no-nonsense robot gunslinger Elle (played by Judd Hamilton, Munro's husband at the time, but voiced in the English language release by Hamilton Camp). We don't know why the cops are chasing them but we do know it's bad enough that they would put their space jalopy in hyperspace gear to avoid getting caught by the law. It works but soon after losing the space pigs they come across the ship that was attacked in the pre-credits scene and its sole survivor. About a minute later the coppers catch up to them again and it's the star slammer for our outlaw heroes.

Of course that was bound to change fast. Sure enough, in the next scene Stella leads a daring prison break that gets everyone else killed (smooth move, Ex-Lax) but rather than face a stiffer sentence or even the death penalty she and Akton are recruited by the Emperor to complete the mission the previous crew died attempting. The evil Count Zarth Arn (Joe Spinell), ruler of the League of Dark Worlds, has created a weapon of such immense destructive power that it needs its own secret planet to reside when not in use. It's up to our duo of charming rogues, joined by Thor and Elle, to find the planet and destroy it and the weapon because Zarth plans to use it to overthrow the Emperor and assume complete control over the universe.

That's usually how these plots go, and that's all the plot we get because the rest of *Star Crash* is Cozzi's laundry list of everything he has ever loved about the movies and wanted to see in one single feature given a pulse. Each planet our heroes travel to has its share of perils, from stop-motion behemoths with swords to an army of Amazon women (ON HORSEBACK!!!) lorded over by their lovely but lethal queen (Nadia Cassini) to a primitive tribe that speaks the language of stark raving shit-nuts, and naturally there has to be a traitor in their midst. The set-pieces get loonier as the threadbare storyline holding it all together barely rockets to a finale that practically defies description.

Somewhere in the thick of it all Hasselhoff makes his entrance in grand style and assumes the dueling duties of dashing hero and potential love interest for Stella despite the fact he doesn't make his first appearance until the third act. Apparently Cozzi never read one of Syd Field's screenwriting books, but that matters little in the end because unlike Field he's a real screenwriter. Traditional storytelling structure means nothing to the director because with *Star Crash* he's basically given us an old-fashioned Republic Pictures serial edited into one breakneck chapter where danger lurks around every corner.

As I mentioned a few paragraphs ago, I currently hold *Star Crash* in much higher esteem than *Star Wars*. There are many reasons for that and they start literally at the beginning. The title *Star Crash* was imposed on Cozzi by his money-hungry producers and it may not have been the one he wanted but it's the one that fits his movie like a glove. What the fuck does it mean? Watch the movie and you'll see. Can you say that about *Star Wars*? That title is dull and pompous and makes me yawn every time I try saying it. *Star Crash* is the rowdy punk rock that lives next door and stays up all night drinking booze and rehearsing the loudest songs they know. I'd rather party with them than hang out with George Lucas at his stiff Sunday afternoon tea.

Usually when you're watching an Italian exploitation flick you can't help but get the sense from most of the actors that they're only in this for the money. Of course you'd be right on. The film industry is a mercenary endeavor that rewards profit and punishes failure. Why shouldn't even our most gifted filmmaking professionals fail to conceal their soul-decaying contempt for the true nature of the business every once in a while? But everyone involved in the making of Star Crash on both sides of the camera looks to be having a complete and utter blast. There's no reason why we shouldn't be doing the same. That kind of fun is not only infectious but rare.

Caroline Munro, the luscious silver screen siren of genre fare, shines brighter than the brightest heavenly body as *Star Crash*'s wide-eyed heroine Stella Star. There's no world-weary cynicism in her character and no hardened exterior to conceal it if it was even there. Stella approaches every adventure with childlike enthusiasm; there are moments when this fearless outlaw who apparently has seen it all is genuinely amazed by the astounding sights she encounters in her mission for the Emperor. She holds her own with the menfolk on the action side of things, but this being an Italian movie Munro has to be rescued from imminent danger about twice as much as she gets to be the badass. Regardless she looks stunning in the skimpy black get-up that has become one of the more iconic visuals in fantastic cinema of the 1970's and Munro captivates every time she's on camera.

It's a real shame that her voice had to be completely dubbed in post-production by actress Candy Clark (*The Man Who Fell to Earth*) since the producers couldn't afford to fly her to the States for ADR. I would have loved to hear her intone some of the crazier lines of dialogue in the gloriously pulpy script Cozzi co-wrote with one of his producers, Nat Wachsberger (Jerry Lewis' unreleased *The Day the Clown Cried*), which pop and crackle (and occasionally snap) with so much wild energy that when matched with the actors' performances often come off like the word balloons you would find in a comic book. Marjoe Gortner, the former evangelist who found his true calling as a B-movie character actor, puts his holy roller charisma and abandon to great use as Stella's mysterious comrade Akton and gets a few of the goofier lines in *Star Crash*, but he says them all with a pleasant smile.

The acting in the original *Star Wars* was serviceable but stiff, made possible mostly by Lucas' disinterest in getting halfway decent performances from his relatively inexperienced cast. "Faster, more intense," was the only direction he was capable of giving the actors hired to bring his vision to life. Luigi Cozzi didn't have that problem at all; he chose performers with talent and enthusiasm to spare, suited them up, and turned them loose. That's how it's done my friends. George C. Scott once spoke of a "joy of performing" that separated the great actors from the good ones. Most of the cast of *Star Crash* seems to embody that rare quality, with Joe Spinell and Christopher Plummer being the standouts.

Spinell is a demented delight as the unhinged villain Zarth Arn, a maniacal monster who could give Doctor Doom the creeps. It's a real to-the-cheap-seats performance in the grand tradition of the cackling deviants who used to oppose the heroes of 1930's and 40's adventure serials. Hired to work for one day at a cost of $10,000, the legendary Plummer refuses to phone in his performance as the Emperor and he makes every line of magnificent expository dialogue given to him by Cozzi just sing to the heavens with a theatrical flair that only one of the great Shakespearean actors of this century could muster. He even gets the single best line of dialogue in the screenplay: "You know, my son, I wouldn't be Emperor of the Galaxy if I didn't have a few powers at my disposal. Imperial Battleship, halt the flow of time!" David Hasselhoff's role is smaller than he would be used to playing in later years but at least he makes his every moment on screen count and even with limited screen time he still gets the girl at the end. Why? Because he's the fucking Hoff baby!

Star Crash may run a lean hour-and-a-half but Cozzi makes every moment count. Once the movie gets going it never pauses for a breath. It sprints from one insane mission to the next with the energy and confidence of a long distance marathon champion. It's a gonzo rollercoaster ride and Cozzi's direction really puts the "opera" in space opera. The greatest Italian filmmakers—Leone, Antonioni, Argento, Bertolucci, Fulci, and Visconti to name but a few—were always master stylists, and the emperor of the cinematic universe of Star Crash makes his film a feast for every sense. Characters get shot and die in slow motion, fight scenes are messy and uncoordinated but still kick ass, spaceships battle it out amidst star fields that twinkle with the colors of a glorious Christmas lighting display, and mythological beasts made flesh through the power of stop-motion animation menace our heroes. In short, you could play this movie with the sound off (and most people would probably prefer to) and the movie would still be fun to watch.

Star Wars is justifiably hailed as a ground-breaker in the advance of modern visual effects, with its fascinating alien creatures and dazzling space battles, but it's also a very drab and depressingly

designed film at times. The story takes place on dour sand planets, inside spaceships that look about as much fun to ride in as taking a cross-country road trip with Mitt Romney, and a planetoid-sized space station that resembles a pinball left on the railroad tracks for a few days. *Star Crash* is set on fantastic worlds with stop-motion animated goliaths that shoot gigantic swords at our heroes and lost planets that host destructive weapons that would make the Death Star look like a bright and noisy toy gun you'd buy at Dollar General for your nephew's eighth birthday.

The spaceships look like they were assembled from plastic model kits—because they were—but that only adds to the movie's high entertainment. Credit is due to the great Armando Valcauda, who had previously worked on the "Spectorama 70" colorization process for Cozzi's 1977 reedited Italian release of the original *Godzilla*, and Germano Natali (Suspiria) for making the visual effects of *Star Crash* as memorable as they are.

Roberto D'Ettorre Piazzoli, who later shot James Cameron's first movie as director *Piranha II: The Spawning* as well as other exploitation faves *The Raiders of Atlantis* and *Sonny Boy*, collaborated with Englishman Paul Beeson (who handled additional photography duties on the first three *Indiana Jones* movies and *Who Framed Roger Rabbit?* and served as second unit director on David Fincher's directorial debut *Alien 3*) on the vibrant, candy-colored cinematography that makes every image come alive. Production designer Aurelio Crugnola created a universe that was comic book in appearance and realistic in texture and would go on to create modest visual miracles on a low budget for Enzo G. Castellari's *The Inglorious Bastards* and Richard Fleischer's *Ashanti* before turning to art direction duties on the multiple Oscar-winning *The English Patient* years later. The swift pacing of the non-stop action sequences is maintained throughout *Star Crash* by ace editor Sergio Montanari (*Django*).

In the end though, *Star Crash* is the lovechild of Luigi Cozzi, and everyone else was just there to help. Cozzi's love of classic science-fiction and fantasy is what gives the movie its ability to transcend the passage of time. He's not in this for the money, but for the sheer thrill of filmmaking. The art of creating a work of cinema that is unique in many ways energized the young director and he packed in everything he ever wanted to see in a fantastic space adventure in *Star Crash*, then he moved on. There was an unofficial *Star Crash 2* that was in fact a retitling of Bitto Albertini's lackluster *Escape from Galaxy 3*, but Cozzi had the good sense to leave the world of Stella Star behind forever after making his one feature.

Unlike George Lucas, who realized after some time that *Star Wars* was his destiny and nothing else, Cozzi moved on to make shamelessly entertaining movies like *Contamination* (renamed *Alien Contamination* for its U.S. release), *Vampire in Venice*, and two *Hercules* flicks for Cannon Films starring Lou Ferrigno. Eventually he retired from directing in order to run Dario Argento's movie memorabilia store *Profundo Rosso* in Italy, but the world of fantastic cinema is all the worse off for it. Yeah, *Star Crash* is one of my favorite movies bar none. Give it a chance and it might become one of yours as well.

"GO FOR HYPERSPACE!"

CRIMINALLY INSANE
THE LEAST POLITICALLY-CORRECT SLASHER FILM

Nick Phillips had been churning out his brand of erotica since 1963 with *Nudes on Credit*. *Pleasures of a Woman*, *The Exotic Mister Rose*, *Roxanna*, and *Dr. Christina of Sweden* among others. Nick incorporated fetish lingerie, bondage gear, and "have sex and meet a terrible end" in his films.

When I did an interview with Nick, I asked why his films had downbeat endings. His answer was that "life, itself, has a downbeat ending; we all die, don't we?" Hard to argue with that king of logic. Nick is the son of one of the first Road Show guys, S.S. Millard. Dad never wanted Nick to get into the business, but once the film bug bites you, it doesn't want to let go.

About 1975 Hollywood was incorporating nudity and sex in mainstream films. Actually it started earlier than that, but XXX features were still attracting crowds. But like David Friedman, HG Lewis, David Durston and other adult film makers, Nick would try his hand at horror, something he really wasn't into. Nick would make a double bill that made the rounds of the Grindhouses and Drive-Ins: *Criminally Insane* and *Satan's Black Wedding*.

Norman Bates may have been the first mad slasher, but who came next? Michael Myers? Jason? Freddy Kruger? No, actually it was a woman. Meet Crazy, Fat Ethel, 250 pounds of maniacal fury. Ethel doesn't kill for money, sex, or drugs. Just don't get between her and her next meal.

The story begins in the local nut house, er, rehabilitation facility. We get an inside look at Ethel's treatments like injections and shock treatments. Ethel is released in the custody of her Grandmother. The doctor assures that everything will be fine as long as Ethel takes her meds and sticks to her diet.

The look on Ethel's face is that the doctor can stick his diet up his ass.

The first day home, Ethel makes a light breakfast, a dozen eggs, a pound of bacon and a loaf of toast. Granny is less than thrilled when a week's worth of groceries is consumed in five minutes. When Ethel gets up for a midnight snack, she finds the edibles have been locked up. Undaunted, she takes a butcher knife and tries to hack open the pantry. All of this noise wakes up Granny. Granny tells Ethel to go back to bed or she'll call the doctor. Ethel rams the knife into Granny's back and it pops out her chest. Ethel dumps Granny's corpse in her own bedroom.

A new day dawns and our mammoth of mayhem is out of chow. She calls the local grocer for an order, but is told that there is an $80 balance from the last order. Ethel agrees to pay and asks for the usual weeks' worth of groceries plus four gallons of ice cream. The delivery boy arrives, but with orders to get the money before turning over the food. Ethel, enraged, grabs the nearest bottle and breaks it over his head. Then stabs him repeatedly with the broken bottle. She dumps his body in Granny's room, then has lunch.

A visitor arrives, an unwelcome one at that. Who would have guessed that our portly predator had a sister? Rosalee is a sleazy looking hooker type, reminiscent of the ones that used to roam around my home turf, offering oral satisfaction for a mere $10 a pop. Ah, memories, memories, but I digress. Rosalee informs our beloved behemoth that she will be staying for a few days and might entertain a friend or two. During this conversation, Ethel polishes off an entire layer cake.

Rosalee bring home a sweaty drunk. Upon seeing Ethel, he asks if she's the Madame. Rosalee turns the trick. She wakes up and notices a foul odor. Wearing a nightgown that looks like it was purchased at Fredrick's of Newark, she asks Ethel is she smells anything. Ethel says no, but Rosalee insists that the smell is coming from granny's room. Rosalee leaves for a bit. Ethel realizes a potential problem exists. She decides to bury granny in the back yard, but the ground is too rocky. She returns to Granny's room with several bottle of Airwick, something I found extremely funny. She leave them in strategic locations to kill the smell.

Rosalee is tricking at a bar when she runs into her ex-boyfriend, er, pimp, John (how original). This film is populated by the most unattractive people ever to grace the Silver Screen. John is your typical '70s white trash pimp. He is one slimy-looking bastard. He cons her into taking him home and gets her in bed. She asks him, "If you love me why did you beat me?" John says, "You need a good beating now and then, all women do." So much for being PC in the '70s. Damn, I miss those days. Say whatever you want with no repercussions. What the fuck happened to this country anyway? Yeah, here I go again, better hit the bong so I can keep it together.

The next day our caloric-challenged cutie has another unexpected visitor, her shrink. Squeezing past Ethel, a feat in itself, he asks her why she hasn't showed up for her treatments. She mutters something and heads upstairs. The shrink follows and gets his head caved in by large candlestick swung by a very pissed off behemoth. The hammering noise of metal meeting skull  wakes up Rosalee, who makes a halfhearted investigation. Seeing nothing, she goes back to bed with her greasy boyfriend.

Breakfast with Ethel is not cool as the boyfriend, John, starts to bait her, to the dismay of Rosalee. Ethel is having a dozen sweet rolls with her coffee. John asks for one with the snide comment, "Are you sure you can spare one?" Rosalee and John start sucking face while Ethel watches TV and consumes a huge bowl of ice cream. Hard to say what was more disgusting, them making out or her eating. The two snort some coke, telling Ethel that the drug is sinus medicine from the doctor.

The doorbell rings and it's a cop looking for the delivery boy. Ethel blows him off, then opens the window in Granny's room to air it out. We see three putrefied bodies on the floor. Rosalee and John really start complaining about the stink. When John threatens to break down the door, Ethel assures them Granny should be back tomorrow. Ethel waits until Rosalee and John are asleep, then hacks them to death with a huge cleaver in the bloodiest scene in the film. John tries to escape, but Ethel follows him, giggling, cleaver in hand, as she hacks at his head.

Ethel dumps the bodies in bed and, starting to hallucinate, runs toward the camera with a large knife. She is hacking up a mannequin and washes the blood off the cleaver. More frightening is Ethel running though a park in slow motion. Maybe this caused that earthquake back in, oh, never mind. Ethel is laughing insanely during this sequence. The drunk that Rosalee brought to the house returns looking for some trim. Pushing Ethel aside, he goes into the murder room with Ethel in pursuit. Freezing when he spots the stacked up corpses, Ethel wrestles him to the floor, choking the life out of him and grunting like she is having an orgasm.

A police detective, uncredited character actor George "Buck" Flower, knocks on the door and questions her about the missing delivery boy. Our hefty heroine puts herself in a bind when she is caught in an obvious lie when she blames his disappearance on a "colored guy", a comment that drew a lot of snickers from the mostly black audience. Now she has to take action. Chopping the bodies up, she puts them in a sack and drives to the ocean. Too many people are around, so she drives back to the house.

She drags the sack into the house, but forgets to close the trunk. A nosey neighbor looks in the trunk and sees a severed hand. The police arrive and find Ethel eating one of the bodies. We see Ethel's blood smeared face as 'The End "appears on the screen and is obscured by a pool of blood. Not a bad film despite its low budget constraints. Ethel is a formidable slasher and the gore effects, while low tech, are very effective. Priscilla Alden as Ethel, plays the role pretty deadpan during most of the film. She is fun to watch as she goes completely berserk in the murder scenes. Alden returned in *Crazy Fat Ethel 2* which was mostly footage from the first film. She did *Death Nurse 1 & 2* for Nick which went straight to VHS on the Chop 'Em Up Video label. Alden passed away in 2007 She appeared on the TV, *Nash Bridges* as Nurse Ratchet in 1997. Nick Phillips is alive and well and living in Las Vegas.

From ALIENS to ZOMBIES: cinemawasteland.com

Cinema Wasteland

THOUSANDS of B-MOVIE, HORROR, SCIENCE FICTION, SPAGHETTI WESTERN, X-RATED & BLAXPLOITATION MOVIE POSTERS! RARE and OUT-OF-PRINT DVDs, COLLECTIBLES, AUTOGRAPHS and Much, Much, More!

The Cinema Wasteland MERCHANDISE CATALOG contains Thousands of Horror, Cult, and "B" Movie related Items. One can be yours for ONLY $3.00 (USA & Canada) or $5.00 Foreign.
Cinema Wasteland   PO Box 8   Berea, OH. 44017
Phone (440) 891-1920   e mail: zombies@cinemawasteland.com
SECURE ON LINE ORDERING AT: cinemawasteland.com

SERVING THE COLLECTOR SINCE 1987

America's PREMIER Drive-In & Grindhouse Movie and Collectible Show!

Cinema Wasteland
MOVIE AND MEMORABILIA EXPO
OCTOBER 2nd, 3rd & 4th, 2015
Holiday Inn   15471 Royalton Rd.   Cleveland, OH. 44136

LEATHERFACE: TEXAS CHAINSAW MASSACRE 3 25TH ANNIVERSARY REUNION

JEFF BURR - Director
"The SAW is Family"

R. A. MIHAILOFF - "Leatherface"
KATE HODGE - "Michelle"
WILLIAM BUTLER - "Michelle"
JENNIFER BANCO - "Leatherface's Daughter"

ADDITIONAL GUESTS TO BE ANNOUNCED

Other GUESTS Will Include:

SUZANNA LEIGH
THE DEADLY BEES, LUST FOR A VAMPIRE, THE LOST CONTINENT, SON OF DRACULA, etc.

KAY PARKER
Golden Age Adult Actress: DRACULA SUCKS, SEX WORLD, TABOO, etc.

TOM SULLIVAN
EVIL DEAD Animator, Effects & Artist.

MOVIES! GUESTS! VENDORS! EVENTS!

THE WASTELAND FILM FEST FEATURES 16mm DRIVE-IN FILMS and INDEPENDENT MOVIES ALL WEEKEND LONG!

SHOP OUR VENDORS ROOM! IT'S A SHOPPING EXPERIENCE LIKE NO OTHER FOR B-MOVIE FANS!

OVER 60 HOURS OF MOVIES, EVENTS and PROGRAMMING!

PANELS, GUEST TALKS, Q&A SESSIONS, SPECIAL EVENTS, and LIVE ENTERTAINMENT!

VENDOR and GUEST ROOM HOURS:
Fri. Oct. 2nd: Doors Open 5pm. Vendor Room Closes 10pm
Sat. Oct. 3rd: Doors Open 10am. Room Closes 7pm.
Sun. Oct. 4th: Doors Open 11am. Shows Colese 5pm.
3-Day Pass Holders admitted at 4:30pm on Friday.
Movies and Events Run until 2am Friday & Saturday Nights.

ADMISSION:
SINGLE DAY: $15 per day until 6/19/15.
3-DAY V.I.P. PASS:
$35 until 6/19/15.
$40 until 9/11/15.

Cinema Wasteland
PO Box 8
Berea, OH. 44017
Phone: (440) 891-1920
zombies@cinemawasteland.com

See our web site for driving directions. Dealer space is sold out, but waiting list is open. Hotel Reservations can be made by calling the Holiday Inn at 1-877-408-4913. Free Parking for all convention attendees.

Don't Miss Either of our CINEMA WASTELAND MOVIE AND MEMORABILIA EXPO'S for 2016!
April 1st, 2nd and 3rd, 2016 * Sept. 30th, Oct. 1st and 2nd, 2016

UP-TO-DATE SHOW AND GUEST INFORMATION CAN BE FOUND ON OUR WEB SITE! cinemawasteland.com

RAW FORCE
ONE OF THE LAST GREAT EXPLOITATION EPICS

The early '80s were the beginning of the end for 42nd Street as I knew it. The AIDS epidemic had started, crack became the cheap drug of choice, making its users Romeroesque zombies ripping off the unwary, and the land grab by greedy, politically connected realtors. The grindhouse, smut emporiums, gay bath houses, porn theaters, and certain bars were closing on a daily basis. All of these factors made the "Deuce "far more dangerous than it had ever been. But the films, the life blood of the grindhouse, kept on coming.

In 1982 a film showed up that was tailor made for the jaded Time Square audience. The film had Kung Fu zombies, cannibals, Piranhas, a Hitler lookalike, pirates, shoot-outs every five minutes, nudity, and Cameron Mitchell. That film was *Raw Force,* aka *Kung Fu Cannibals*. It played at a theater that showed three different Kung Fu films every week. The theater was right in the middle of the "Deuce", in close proximity to the notorious porn emporium, Blackjack Books. I can't recall the name of the place as it wasn't a theater I frequented. I wasn't a big fan of these imported, badly dubbed, chop-socky epics. Oh, I did see the classics like *Five Fingers of Death*, the Bruce Lee Films, and *Five Deadly Venoms*. But that was it. The only other times I would go to this place was to see oddball Asian films like *Killer Snakes, Black Magic* and *Lady Terminator*.

Raw Force's one sheet poster sucked me in. For once, the film delivered what it promised, 90-minutes of complete mayhem. Shot in the Philippines, it opens with a group of thugs, led by a guy with a German accent and a Hitler mustache, trading a bunch of Asian girls for huge chunks of jade. The girls are traded to a sect of monks living on Warrior Island, a place where disgraced martial artists are sent to die. The girls are weighed and their weight is given to the thugs in jade. One girl is too skinny, so the monks don't want her. The thugs leave her and she is turned into sushi by weird looking specter with a samurai sword.

Hazel Buck is running a cruise ship that looks more like a tramp steamer. The crusty Captain Harry Dobbs (Mitchell) is the skipper. Hazel is taking a bunch of martial artists to tour Warrior Island. A couple of the men on the tour decide to visit a whorehouse before leaving. The Hitler guy has picked that particular whorehouse to raid for girls. He strikes up a conversation with one of the guys, then sees the brochure for the trip to Warrior Island. He advises them not to go. The whorehouse is raided by phony cops and girls are hauled away. Look for Camille Keaton and Jewel Sheppard in this scene.

The Hitler guy can't let this ship get to Warrior Island and expose his deal with the monks. The monks eat the girls and that give them the power to raise the dead fighters. In the dead of night, the gang pirates the cruise ship and a bloody battle breaks out. People are diced up with swords, shot with arrows, guns etc. It's a massacre and the ship is set ablaze. The Captain, Mrs Buck and some of the martial artists escape in a lifeboat. They wind up on Warrior Island with the thugs in pursuit. An insane shootout in a cemetery decimates the ranks of the thugs. The monks find the group and offer them some island hospitality. The girls are grabbed and are being prepared for dinner. The guys rescue them and are told they now have to battle the resurrected fighters to get off the island. This fight had the patrons of the theater going nuts.

The Hitler guy and a couple of his men have loaded so much jade into the plane that it sinks in piranha infested waters and the Hitler guys becomes dinner. The survivors hold off the Kung Fu zombies and escape Warrior Island. The film ends with "To Be Continued" which it wasn't. After its brief run, *Raw Force* wound up as regular programming on the early days of HBO. It got a VHS release on Media Home Entertainment.

Other than Cameron Mitchell, who had become a fixture in bad, grade Z '80s films, there are no "name" stars. Jillian Kesner was the blonde, "Cookie Winchell", and actually a legit martial artist. She had been in *Student Bodies*, where she met her future husband, noted cinematographer, Gary Graver. She was also in *Firecracker, Beverly Hills Vamp* and she was Fonzie's girlfriend, Lorraine in TV's *Happy Days*. She and Gary Graver were trying to complete Orson wells unfinished film, *The Other Side of the Wind*. Graver died in 2006 at age 68 from cancer. Jillian continued her effort to preserve Welles' legacy, but died in 2007 from a staph infection. She was 58.

Others appearing in *Raw Force* had either been on TV series or a couple of other films. Cameron Mitchell continued to appear in every kind of low budget genre film like *Blood Link, Low Blow, Mission Kill, Mutant War, The Offspring*, plus a lot of TV appearances. He died in 1994 at age 75. Stuntman and actor, Gary Kent, credits Mitchell with giving him his start.

Raw Force is one of those rare exploitation films that actually delivers what it promises. And what would any Philippino film be without Vic Diaz? Look for Vic as one of the monks. CAV finally released a nice-ish looking *Raw Force* on Blu-Ray in October, 2014. So now you have no excuse.

WITHOUT WARNING
THE FILM THAT BECAME THE TEMPLATE FOR PREDATOR

A lot of people thought 1987's *Predator* was an original idea. It wasn't; the settings just changed. *Without Warning* was an alien hunter in rural America. *Predator* was set in the South American jungles. *Predator* boasted a testosterone fueled cast: Arnold Swartzanagger, Carl weathers, Sonny Landon, Bill Duke and Jesse Ventura. *Without Warning* seemed to have a cast culled from central casting's unemployment line. Not that this was a bad thing as Jack Palance, Martin Landau, Cameron Mitchell, Ralph Meeker, Neville Brand, David Caruso and even Larry Storch were cast in the film.

In another strange twist, the almost seven-foot-tall, Kevin Peter Hall, was cast as the creature in both films. Action fans may say that *Predator* is the better film. Maybe in terms of better effects, but as far as capturing a combination of sleazy horror and sci fi elements, *Without Warning* was creepier and nastier. Shot in what looks like a barren section of wilderness, you get a weird feeling from the get-go that something is wrong. Strange small creatures seem to come out of nowhere. The alien throws these things at its prey and they burrow through their victims. Kind of like the flying fingers from *It Conquered the World*. *Predator* used a flying metal contraption to kill some of its trophies.

Jack Palance is Taylor, a gas station owner and a former big game hunter who is aware of what's going on. Martin Landau is "Sarge", a shell shocked veteran who knows there is something out there. Creepy music plays over the credits as a hunter (Cameron Mitchell) and his wimpy son are up early to hunt. The hunter mocks his son as a sissy and makes him come along with him. The hunter is struck with two flying creatures that start to burrow though him. He crawls to his son, who also gets attacked.

A van with two couples stops at a decrepit gas station. They meet Sarge and the gas station owner, Taylor who warn them something may be amiss in the woods. They ignore that advice. A scout master (Larry Storch) is leading a pack of Cub Scouts. When he leaves the boys to grab a smoke, he is taken out by the flying creatures. Sandy and Craig (Tarah Nutter and Chris Nelson) leave Tom & Beth (David Caruso and Lynn Theel) to get busy. When they return, the two are gone. A search leads them to a shed where they find their friends dead and hanging on hooks with the other victims.

The couple takes off as one of the flying creatures starts to eat its way through the windshield. They go to a roadhouse full of barflies. Neville Brand and Ralph Meeker are the main patrons. When told of the killings, they call Sarge, who is shooting pool. Sarge knows of the alien, but thinks the couple have been taken over by alien forces. When the power goes out, Sarge flips out and shoots the Sheriff by accident. Taylor finds the couple and has them take him to the shed. Taylor knows the creature will come back for its trophys, so he sets a trap with explosives. One of the flying Frisbees gets on Taylor's leg. Sandy and Craig take off for help.

Taylor peels the creature off his leg with a knife. The couple flag down a police car, but Sarge is driving it. Craig tries to placate Sarge by telling him yes, they are aliens and these are the invasion plans. This catches Sarge off guard and the two escape to an abandon home. Craig tells Sandy to get some rest. When she wakes up she finds Craig dead and the Alien in the house. Taylor shows up and empties his rifle into the alien with no effect. Taylor and Sandy go back to the shed, knowing the alien will follow. They are just about to blow it up when Sarge appears and is killed by the flying creatures. Taylor, now mortally wounded, has to get the creature into the shed. He goes into the shed, but the Alien starts to go after Sandy. Taylor grabs its leg and holds it as Sandy sets off the dynamite.

Without Warning was released in 1980. Grindhouses and Drive In were in their death throes about then. Major film companies had started stealing elements from these low budget films. In a few years, films like Without Warning would bypass theaters and go directly to VHS. The reported budget for the film was $150,000 of which $75,000 was Jack Palance and Martin Landau's salaries. The two were reunited in 1982 for another low budget horror film, *Alone in the Dark*. Reportedly Palance wasn't happy doing these films and went on a tirade on set. Landau, however, took it all in stride and was a convincing loonie in both films. Landau made one more low-budget turd for Jackie Kong, *The Being*. Both actors, later on, won an Oscar for best Supporting Actor. Jack Palance for *City Slickers* and Martin Landau for *Ed Wood*.

Other actors in *Without Warning* were at the ends of their respective careers. This was Ralph Meeker's last film. Meeker had been a busy character actor for decades appearing in A-films like *Paths of Glory, The Dirty Dozen*, and *The St. Valentine's Day Massacre*. He also was in Bert Gordon's *Food of the Gods* and Greydon Clark's *Hi Riders*. He died in 1988. Neville Brand did two more films before his death in 1992, *The Return* and *Evils of the Night*. Brand was one of the most highly decorated veterans of WWII. Larry Storch is still working today.

As for the younger members of the cast, Tarah Nutter did a few TV shows and hasn't been heard from since 1988. According to those in the know, she was a real bitch to deal with. David Caruso went on to stardom with Abel Ferrara's *King of New York* and the TV shows, *China Girl* and *NYPD Blue* (a sweet gig he completely blew by pulling a McLean Stevenson, leaving and trying for superstardom before returning to TV for *CSI: Miami*, where he puts sunglasses on. A lot.). Christopher Nelson had done a lot of TV before *Without Warning*. He also appeared *in T.A.G.: The Assassination Game* and *The Pink Motel*. He is the son of actor Ed Nelson. Lynn Theel was in *Humaniods from the Deep* and *Hollywood Boulevard II*. She hasn't been seen since 1990.

Without Warning was picked up for distribution by AIP. Before it was released, AIP was bought out by Filmways, a company that had no desire to release low budget films. As a result, it got limited play in major markets, but developed a cult following from guys like me who actually got to see it. It is slated for an official release from Shout! Factory as of this writing.

INTERVIEW WITH SCOTT MAYER
'SAVAGE STREETS' PAVED WITH GOOD INTENTIONS

By: Dr. Rhonda Baughman

Savage Streets will never die, actually—because right now, it really is 'Red's turn'.

Cult/exploitation aficionados worth the weight of their VHS and poster collections know to watch Savage Streets in hushed (or boisterous) reverence. The rabid fans out there, then, have reviewed the film online, reviewing the plot, quoting dialogue, and posting Youtube videos in dedication ecstasy. Some lucky fans even made it to the 2013 California Monsterpalooza *Savage Streets* reunion and will make it to the (Maine) Coast City Comicon in November 2013. The 'Destroy All Movies' folks most likely have the best review ever written, anyway—and I will double check that data when I leave Tucson, AZ to return to my copy patiently waiting for me in my Canton, OH storage unit.

And then there's just little me—Hurricane Rhonda. Chainsaw to closer associates. I am working on that level of dedication above, but in the meantime, as only a voracious fan. I will instead play several songs from the Savage Streets soundtrack, on the vinyl copy I own, gritty-sounding now even with careful storage, purchased in my lost youth from the way-defunct Camelot Music and then Skype Scott 'Red' Mayer at 8am PST before all corporate America gibberish begins.

Most reviews of Savage Streets I've read seem to focus on plot recaps and summaries, as well as surface level analysis, and pay close, repeated attention to the rape scene, tits in general, and the "bad" acting. Those are all worthy items to discuss, so I will note that:

According to Mayer, the rape scene was the first he shot for production.

Tits are nice. I have them. But I am confused, however, as to the seemingly endless debate for either the extreme controversy cupping them or the fanatical obsession massaging them. (There's also the tiny camp who have no idea what they're for, but that's a different article.) With that, I will add that I think they are used correctly, on all counts, in *Savage Streets*.

"Bad" is a relative term, of course and a painfully boring adjective. One man's 'bad' might be another's 'brilliant exercise in cinematic bloom'! Mostly, I've moved on from simple terms such as 'bad', 'neat', 'good', 'suck', 'rawk', 'hawt', and I will never embrace text speak nor comments on the internet from illiterate, passive-aggressive, and anonymous online dwellers.

The film is what it is ... and even those engaging in early level literary criticism such as reader-response theory, will, at the very least, offer the 'why' of the reaction and offer credible illustrations and proof.

So, I'm only Rhonda Run-On and Endless Exposition for one reason:

This film is, and always has been, extremely important to me—now and as the 9 year old with her own pink laminated way-defunct Video Time rental card, zipping about and consistently renting the same inappropriate movies over and over(myriad reasons, most harmless, I can state). *Savage Streets* represented the intensity of music, punk fashion, punk portrayal, cheerleaders, not giving a fuck about following the in-crowd, cruelty, love, the gritty Hollywood scene, Linnea Quigley, and sweet, sweet motherfucking vengeance. I might have been only 9, but even I knew the film wasn't just about boobies and rape.

When I return to Ohio, I am going to throw my own *Savage Streets*-themed party, spinning the vinyl soundtrack alone, if I have to—and I will consider it the social event of my season.

INTERVIEW WITH SCOTT MAYER

"Honestly, I never believed after 30 years people would still be interested in *Savage Streets*. I didn't even know until I was signed up for a Facebook account," Mayer tells me via our Skype interview on September 20th, 2013.

I explain to Mayer my early youth, the only child, introvert syndrome—and he understands.

"I also have raised an only child—and we've actually raised her to do whatever she wants to do. We have an open door for her any time she needs us, or has questions. Miranda, my daughter, is 15 years old, extremely self-motivated and independent and the lead vocalist/bass player for her own band, Imagination's Playground. She's badass, I have to admit. We also raised her in a gender neutral fashion. These days, I think girls still need to be told they can do whatever they want to do—and I wanted my daughter to know that, to know all avenues were open to her, and we would support her no matter what," says Mayer.

There's a slight visual delay on my Skype video, but I hope he can see how vigorously I am nodding my head.

Mayer was pleased with an interview he completed for the 2-disc DVD release of *Savage Streets* but was actually unaware that's where the interview was going."It was really the farthest thing from my mind that anything related to *Savage Streets* would even resurface. And then bang! One day on Facebook, I connected with Rich Clement, the man mostly responsible for [finding and assembling many of the less active industry cast members] for the 30 year reunion at Monsterpalooza.

Scott is actually the son of industry veteran Ken Mayer (Space Patrol, Gunsmoke, Bonanza, et al)—a fact I actually did not know before the interview. So, really, here I was watching Mayer's father also in my early youth (reruns with my mother, in case my teen students are reading this and do not understand I'm not actually of the Baby Boomer generation) only to come full circle to interview the son. It's days like today I really love being a writer.(And one day, I hope to be able to be able to treat a film review with the same consuming and detailed research abilities like author Mike Watt does in Fervid Filmmaking-66 Cult Pictures of Vision, Verve and No Self-Restraint.)

I want to know how Mayer was treated on set, since his IMDB profile lists *Savage Streets* as his first and only acting credit, but in fact, as I also find out in the interview, Mayer had already broken into the business via major corporation national commercials. I also want to know if the glittery showbiz bug bit him because of his pop.

"I was treated well, of course, but a little differently. I really was a punk, actually, an art rocker. Anything girls liked to see me dressed in, I wore it," Mayer laughs."I lived on Cherokee Street, about a block from Hollywood Blvd. So, the Hollywood scene was really just my thing at the time. I saw all the bands and made friends with those around me—I mean, I had street pals, junkie roommates, musician buddies, transgender scream-and-yell across the street to each other friends. I rented the entire second floor of this 1930s building for $600.00/month. We threw parties all the time."

I tell Scott the truth—that although I have many of these same types of friends and whole lot more I would simply call 'civilians', it's all in the 2013 sense. That anyone who understands my love of the world, before the year 2001, and my close associates' loathing of the current culture—also understands how jealous we all are at hearing this story. And because we know there are many, many more like it.

"I knew the building was going to be leveled in two years, so I wanted to experience everything and anything I could. It was actually a priority at the time, I would say," Mayer continues."I should have been more active in the industry, gone to more actor and producer parties, but I didn't want to hang out with those people. There's nothing wrong with those people, especially quite a few who were trying to help me along, but I just had my own set of priorities. I wanted to see what it was like to live on the grittier side, and I did. And from my living quarters, I could walk to all the best clubs. The club scene we shot for the film, it was a real club we used to go to in downtown LA. It's been a few years, so I can't recall the name of the club, nor who the gentlemen were onstage in the film. I remember being so excited to shoot there, since the music featured there really represented the scene I was into at the time."

"My father was an amazing man, very supportive, and a real veteran—a character actor for over 45 years. I have acting in my blood, certainly, but my father left the door open—not discouraging, not encouraging, but allowing me to decide what I wanted to do. I was in many plays when I was younger and one day I went with my father to his agent's office, who represented many commercial actors, as well. And I just did it. I played the alternative guy in commercials for Chunky Candy Bar, McDonald's, Suzuki, Miller Light. The Miller Light commercial played during the Superbowl even, so you know I made a pretty good living between the ages of 21-23 and I didn't have to work, I just went on auditions. I just don't think I had the high-level of passion to hustle—I didn't really want it. I had a good time, but it wasn't my only focus," says Mayer.

And if there were ever truer words spoken that I could relate to about acting, I'm not really sure what they would be.

Mayer continues, "In my 20s, I felt different from my friends. The alternative dress I loved was just beginning. I pierced my septum before, you know, it was a commonplace cultural item. I was extreme for the time, but decided to back off slightly when I could see mothers shielding their children from me. In Northern California, no one gives a second look anymore to alternative dress or pierced anything. Sadly," Scott says sarcastically," unless you're wearing a head scarf, head dress of some sort, a hijab, no one cares how you look or even looks twice."

He's right. It's 2013, so I'm not sure either why this is an issue.

"In my dad's time," Mayer says, "all of the actors helped each other, at least among his friends. Auditions, job leads, they let each other know of these things. It was critical to compete, but not cutthroat like it is now, and like it wasn't even for me in the early '80s. I mean, I remember auditioning for a part on a soap opera, and one actor deliberately handed me an old script, knowing I didn't know there were rewrites."

Cutthroat, I agree, but not many murder attempts or smashed kneecaps.

"As an oddball on the set, though, overall I think I was treated well, I just don't think most people knew how to take me. I was low-key and professional on set, but I do have a sense of humor and like to joke on set to release tension. Someone else did apparently, too—the fake marijuana was switched for the real thing during the bleacher scenes, when the Scars are checking out the cheerleaders and spot Linnea's character. So, I was actually very stoned during that scene," Mayer laughs.

And I thought my jealousy had simple bounds, I say.

"Don't be jealous—Red loves you all!"

I feel a little better.

"I got along with everyone on set, too. Only Sal scared me, really. I never knew what was coming next from that guy. Neither did anyone else. He was spontaneous to an extreme. I could never tell if he was a real hood or an actor. He's doing great things now, though, teaching acting and doing lots of movies and television."

Mayer questioned, as did many fans, why a 'weirdo' like Red would actually hang out with guys like Jake and Fargo. Vince's character is obvious—he's weak, needs protection, needs to fit in. Perhaps in some ways Red does, too. Or perhaps, as I think, Red is actually the scariest hood of them all—nice at first, only to show extreme and disconnected cruelty later—and how could someone like Linnea's character really see any of it coming? I ask Mayer if the unhinged, giggly element was all him …?

"The giggle is mine, actually. Producer John Strong had a 1950s sensibility for these thugs. He really wanted Red to be the 'weirdo'. The character was all me—no one directed or advised me to act in any way. [Writer/Director} Danny Steinmann just wanted me to know my lines and hit my marks. I loved how I got the role, actually. I was in a nightclub and met a woman who tells me she casts extras, and at that age, with the attitude, of course, I say, 'I don't do extra work, I'm a SAG actor,'" Mayer laughs, "but I go to the roundtable the next day to read for *Savage Streets*. And at our original roundtable, Cherie Curie was reading for Linda Blair's role, actually."

"At Linnea's reading, I remember seeing other fake punks, with ridiculous faux hawks and goofy styles and I couldn't help but think 'Look at these lame asses! I can do this so much better!' I had that same attitude and decided to just go extreme with it. I lifted Linnea and slammed her on the table—no warning, but I'd had so much theater stunt experience, I knew how to do it without hurting anyone. I got the part on the spot. And then, of course, I apologized. Linnea was very sweet about it. She really is an absolute sweetheart. I wish I had her confidence—back in the day and now."

Mayer is actually thinking about starting his own company—and I, personally, would line up to order a pair of the pants he had in the film, which he can actually make. As a child, I thought the pants were cool. As an adult, you best believe I would unflinchingly purchase and rock those pants.

"I became friends with the costume designer, and eventually even dated another costume designer. It allowed me to do much of what I wanted to do with my look for the film. Except for the hair. The producers and director would not back down on the hair."

"I wasn't given a background story or motivation. The original script was so much different than what the film actually became. The boys, the Scars, become so much more interesting than the girls. The original script wasn't like that. There's a scene that was cut—showing major character development for the boys. Sal playing chess—and he loses, knocks over the table. I'm snorting huge lines of coke, there's a more sensitive side to Jake the audience gets to see, and more of the homoerotic back story—this scene showed where all of that came from. The particular night we shot that scene was truly great. Of course, the fake coke was switched for the real deal. Which is good, actually—the fake coke will give you diarrhea. We shot the lair scene in the factory where we were killed, in a smaller room downstairs—which served as the clubhouse, so to speak. It really was in a shady, dark part of LA and when we weren't shooting Sal and Robert went across the street to the bar—I was never invited, but soon started dating that costume designer, so I didn't feel too badly."

"But in the end … the movie just ran out of money. Checks bounced and we were continually told we would be contacted. A few days went by, a few weeks went by, which turned into months and I became very, very depressed. I had bright copper-colored hair, and didn't really hustle due to the depression, for other auditions, although I did go on them. Finally—we got the call to return to the set, six months later. I had a re-dye and was good to go, while the main money guys were socked with SAG penalties. So, I did receive a nice, fat check for that. And I spent it—oh man, did I spend it—on my Volkswagen Camper. I found the most expensive detailing place in Beverly Hills, and loved that I could park my yellow van next to Cadillacs and I could stand proud in my punk clothes and piercings," Mayer recalls.

"And the good news was, too," Scott continues, "that I could pay back my girlfriend and parents for all the support during the film's hiatus. But I was bummed about the cut scene. The original script was also supposed to feature underground LA bands, but something happened during the hiatus and a different deal was made. The new script cut character development scenes for the girls, too. The gang girl scenes were no longer as prominent. You'll notice in the locker room scene there's gang girl, or two, even, you only see once or twice in the film. I have no clue what happened to all of the rest of their footage."

That actually all makes sense now. I knew some things were amiss, but now that I know of the film's hiatus, those little anomalies poke a little less at the back of my brain.

Mayer confirms that he did indeed ride to the set with Linnea, but had actually forgotten about it until she reminded him.

"She was so much fun to hang with," Scott says, "and I knew almost nothing about her. I just know I felt so bad during the rape scene, so apologetic, and she was just very sweet, very no big deal. I really do wish I had her level of confidence. The rape scene really was the first scene I shot for the film and I felt that my character was established—crazy, seemingly nice guy turns scary. The transition was instant."

"After the film's release, I was stopped on the street a few times, not a lot, nor every day, but a few times I can vividly recall. Mostly asking if I was 'that crazy guy'. I was just so thankful I was recognized, and for a while I felt I was on a roll. I remember going to see the film at an inner-city theater in LA—and it was such a blast, a real joy to see people laughing and talking and yelling at the screen. I recall one patron saying 'Damn! These white people be gettin' crazier every day!'" I laugh alongside Mayer. Yeah, that patron was not wrong—then or now, I say.

"It is weird seeing yourself 20 feet tall on the big screen. It's really humbling. I liked it, but at the same time I was also embarrassed. I had lived no other way, you see. I'd just always been around artists and actors, but something inside me was just not fulfilled. I thought a move to Northern California would be a good idea. I could grow pot, be a hippie, kick back, maintain a nice piece of land. I could always come back, I thought—if I wanted to. Like, it would all just be waiting if I wanted to come back. I just never did. I grew up, got married, went to work, had a child. I love everything I did, for sure, but I have to be honest and say I do have the bug again."

Mayer continues, "I know that if I had stayed in LA, I would have gotten into drugs, for real. And if I started making even more money, I would have had the means to buy all the drugs I wanted. I just didn't trust myself. There were people who were really trying to help me, give me leads, help me continue acting, but I couldn't help thinking it wasn't genuine. Even though now I know it was."

Mayer tells me that Robert Dryer (Jake) has a script. There has been talk and pitches and the idea of *Savage Streets* sequel." We play our fathers," Mayer says, "pissed our sons are dead."

It's brilliant, I think, and just the kind of remake that won't make me cringe, that in fact, would actually get me to the theater or the Redbox, wherever it should land.

I do also want to know about John Vernon—another actor who would pass away before I could stalk him for an interview. I wanted to know if the behind-the-scenes tales I'd heard were true.

"He was an intense professional," Mayer says. "I'm not really sure what he thought of all of us guys. I had met him once before, with my dad, but Vernon didn't remember me. He was kinda grumpy and crusty when we shot our scenes, as was his character, though. He was very curt and I just assumed his mood, his method, depended on the scene, even perhaps how he was feeling."

Sadly, I am among the many who regret missing the Burbank convention, but I have a good feeling there will be another con I do get to where *Savage Streets* cast members wander about and welcome me with open arms and let me stupidly quote dialogue and take photos and sign my VHS copy.

"I had a great time, a really amazing time, actually at the Burbank convention. I loved meeting the fans and everyone was so nice and friendly. It's all so new to me, though, and I was uncomfortable taking money at first. I'm so humble these days. There was nothing wrong with it, it just felt strange to me," Scott says. I confirm what others have told him—that, as fans, we love meeting our idols, taking photos, engaging in conversation, hearing the memories, and actually having the chance to tell those we admire that their art, their contributions, matter.

"All of the fans were great—I especially loved the European female fans who had posters of me on their walls. Teen idol, I had no idea. So far, there's really only been one creepy guy online and a few creepy girls," Mayer says.

That's how you know you've really arrived, I tell him, when the wackos come out.

"I am really interested in people, so I can take the good with the occasionally creepy. I let people play out their story with me, whatever it may be, and I just respond to them. I've felt different all my life, and while not always shunned, shunned enough to know the feeling and that I never want to make anyone feel that way," Mayer admits. "If I could tell the younger me anything, it would be to take opportunities when they present themselves and take advantage of those offers of help when they are extended. Not everyone is out to get you, some folks genuinely do want to help. There were so many opportunities I turned down, not knowing people were really on my side, or for the simple fact I wasn't passionate enough about the path I was on. I would tell that younger me to have more confidence, to pay just a little more attention to the future."

I say go for it, Scott—It's still your turn.

TONY ANTHONY: THE STRANGER
STRANGER IN TOWN & THE STRANGER RETURNS

Fistful of Dollars was a huge success worldwide. Eastwood's "Man With No Name" character was destined to spawn imitations, but none were more blatant than The Stranger Series. Released almost back to back in the States in 1968, Stranger in Town was actually A Dollar in the Teeth directed by Luigi Vanzi. Since the competing United Artists had released the "Dollars" films, MGM was looking to get in on the popularity of the Spaghetti Westerns.

Roger Pettito, from Clarksburg, West Virgina started acting as Tony Anthony in Force of Impulse (1961). He started working in Italy in 1964. He was cast in A Dollar in the Teeth, the film that producer, Alan Klein, picked up and changed to A Stranger in Town. Anthony came off as a low rent version of Eastwood, complete with serape and wise cracks. The tagline for Stranger was "If you got the guts, the gun and the gold, you can make women beg, men die, and a town crawl. '

The Stranger arrives in a Mexican town in time to see bandit, Aguilar (Frank Wolff) massacre a group of Mexican soldiers with a machine gun. Wolff had worked for Roger Corman in *I, Mobster*, *The Wasp Woman* and *Ski Troop Attack*. He was also in the Monte Hellman monster flick, Beast from Haunted Cave. Wolff found better work overseas in Italy. After his performance in Salvatore Giuliano 1962, he was in high demand for Spaghetti Westerns and crime films. Usually cast as Mexican bandit leaders, he did get other roles like the funny sheriff in Corbucci's *The Great Silence* and the doomed Brett McBain in Leone's *Once Upon a Time in the West*. He was also in Fernando DeLio's *Caliber Nine*. Wolff suffered from severe depression and committed suicide in 1971.

After the massacre, the Stranger tells Aguilar that he and his men are worth a lot of bounty money. He makes Aguilar a proposition, a shipment of gold is to be handed over to the Mexican government. Since the officer in charge wouldn't recognize the Mexican captain, he says he will vouch for Aguilar for a cut of the gold. The outnumbered soldiers turn the gold over to Aguilar. Off course Aguilar double crosses the Stranger. He is beaten up and then whipped by Aguilar's dykish side kick, Chica (Jolanda Modio) sporting an early case of western camel toe.

With the help of a girl, The Stranger escapes, gets a shotgun, and takes out Aguilar's men. He faces off with shotgun against machinegun. Although there is a lot of violence, it isn't as convincing or as sadistic as the Leone films it tries to emulate. Anthony isn't really terrible in the role, in fact he sort of eases though it. Wolff had a pedigree in playing villains, so the film is never dull.

Right after this film, another was quickly made. A Man, a Horse and a Gun 1968, became The Stranger Returns. This one up the ante in the violence department. 20 outlaws tree a town in order to rob a gold shipment. The Stranger rides into town after taking the identity of a dead postal inspector he finds on the way. This time the bandits are after a strong box of gold carried in a stagecoach. Actually the stagecoach is made out of the gold. The Stranger endures a few beatings, then teams up with a crazy preacher, borrowing the preacher's four barreled revolving shotgun.

This one has some violence against women including one gunned down and a rape. Jill Banner (*Spider Baby*) is the rape victim. Banner had done a few film, but got a lot of work from Jack Webb for his cop shows like Dragnet. Usually she played a hippie. She was killed by a drunk driver in 1982 at age 35. She had been employed by Marlon Brando, developing scripts for him.

Tony Anthony made one more Stranger film, *Silent Stranger* (1969) aka *The Stranger in Japan*. A dispute with producer Allen Klein made MGM shelve the film and not release it until 1975. Although I have never seen it, those who have reported that it was the best of the series. Anthony returned to the genre in *Blindman* 1971. His delivery of 50 mail order brides to some miners was stolen by his partner. He wants them back and revenge. Rated R, it was more violent and quirky than the Stranger films. Directed with flourish by Fernando Baldi, who had been churning out Sword and Sandal epics and Spaghetti westerns since the '50s. A selling point was casting former Beatle, Ringo Starr as Candy, the head bandit. Starr actually was very good in the role.

Anthony did more films for Baldi. He did *Get Mean* in 1975. Then, in the '80s he brought back 3D films with Com*in at Ya* 1981 and *Treasure of the Four Crowns* 1983. After these films, Anthony left the business, returning occasionally to do production work for Mark Damon and Gene Quintana who were close friends. Thankfully he is still with us as of this writing.

REVIEWS

Bullet to the Head (2013) with Sylvester Stallone, Sung Kang, and Christian Slater. '80s action stars just won't quit. I don't know who looks worse right now, Sly or Arnold. If this wasn't directed by Walter Hill, I would have never picked it up. Stallone, now resembling a wizened Charles Bronson, hey, they were both short, is a hit man in New Orleans. After he and a partner pull a job, another hit man tries to do them in. Stallone teams with a Korean/American cop to make things right.

Goliath and the Barbarians/Goliath and the Vampires (1959-64). Another great double feature from Wild East. Former Tarzan, Gordon Scott is Goliath in both films. Vampires is the one to watch as it was directed by future spaghetti western legend, Sergio Corbucci (*Django, The Great Silence*). For a 60's film, this is a pretty violent and bloody affair. Raiders attack villages, killing the men and carrying off the women. The title vampire drinks the women's blood. One of the women is Goliath's squeeze, so he kicks major ass here. I saw this as part of a Kiddee Matinee back in the day.

The Good, the Bad, and the Weird (2010). Someone really knows his westerns, both American and Spaghetti, Director Kim Jee Woon throws in homages from The Good the Bad and the Ugly to Rio Conchos. Three strangers chase a treasure map across Manchuria in the 30's. Bandits, local gangsters and the Japanese army battle for control of the area. Nonstop gun smoked action from a guy who really did his homework.

Predators (2010) Seems they are going to revive the *Predator* franchise. I thought this was the revival, silly me. Not a bad film as a group of professional killers are transported to a planet to be hunted by the Predators. These guys, however, fight back. The "prey" are Adrien Brody, Lawrence Fishburne, Danny Trejo, Walton Groggins, and Oleg Taktarov. Great action and it was left open for a sequel, but I'm not holding my breath.

Sushi Girl (2012) with Tony Todd, James Duval, Mark Hamill, Danny Trejo, and Jeff Fahey directed by Kern Saxton grabbed this for $1 at Blockbuster's death throes sale. Amazing film and Mark Hamill is way over the top. Revenge with a great twist. Really worth checking out as it's the best thing Tony Todd has done in years. Even if you think Tony sucks, still worth a look.

Godzilla (2014) Ok, thank Christ it wasn't a fuckin iguana' again. But only about 15 minutes of screen time for Big G? And what the fuck happened to his trade mark roar? Two stupid monsters get more screen time and the only time he blows fire is down the other monster's throat—WTF? Where the rampaging Big G of old? Only in this PC era could you make a fire breathing dinosaur a pussy. Showing the incredible dumbing down of America, some people actually believed that in 1954 a huge lizard attacked Tokyo. I need a fuckin bong hit.

Chato's Land (1972) Charles Bronson is Pardon Chato, a half-breed Apache who is forced into a shootout with a bigot sheriff. Jack Palance forms a posse of racists intent on hanging Chato. After raping Chato's woman and killing his son, Chato's extracts bloody vengeance. This wasn't the first time he played an Indian, *Run of the Arrow* (1957), *Never So Few* (1959), and *Guns for San Sebastian* (1968). Two years later Bronson hit it big with *Death Wish*. Directed by Michael Winner.

The Outfit (1973). Robert Duval teams up with Karen Black and Joe Don Baker to avenge his brother's death at the hands of the Outfit. Adapted from the Richard Stark (Donald Westlake) novel and directed by John Flynn, worth watching just for the cast: Timothy Carey, Robert Ryan, Marie Windsor, Richard Jaeckel, Elisha Cook, Sheri North, Bill McKinney, Joanna Cassidy and others.

King Kong vs. Godzilla (1962). After watching the "revision" I had to dig out the only movie I ever stood in line for. This is the Big G that we all love. First in a line of Godzilla vs. big monsters. The formula worked for years and was even used not so long ago as high tech versions were made in Japan, but seldom released here except for a few import DVDS. Still a fun watch after almost 50 years.

Razorback (1983) Arguably the best killer pig movie ever made. The titular creature kills and eats people in the outback. After a lady journalist disappears, her husband arrives looking for answers. Great cinematography, scummy kangaroo hunters, a "pet food "plant and quirky characters all elevate this OZ fest. Directed by Russell Mulcahy.

The Split (1968) From another Richard Stark "Parker" novel, this heist film reunites *Dirty Dozen* alumni Jim Brown, Ernest Borgnine and Donald Sutherland. Big Jim plans a heist at an LA Rams game and assemble a crew including Warren Oates and Jack Klugman. They get $548,000, but the mastermind, Julie Harris, suggests they hide it at Brown's ex-wife's (Diahann Carroll) place. But when creepy landlord (James Whitmore) kills her during an attempted rape, the money vanishes. The crew turns on Brown, but brown finds out an op that he tipped (Gene Hackman) killed the landlord and took the money. The film tanks when Brown and Hackman turn on Brown's crew. Good up until that point.

*****FIVE STAR REVIEWS CAN'T BE WRONG*****

GUNFIGHTERS OF THE DRUNKEN MASTER
by Pete Chiarella aka 42nd Street Pete

After solar flares dry up all the water on the planet, the world is turned into a barren wasteland. Any liquid not stored in a glass or plastic container has been contaminated. There is, however, a lot of liquor, and the wasteland is populated by violent drunks heavily armed with a variety of weapons. The baddest of the bad is the Drunken Master, who rules the area with an iron fist. But one fateful day, he wasn't bad enough. In a battle with the notorious El Roacho Rio, his gun hand is crippled. The Master put a bounty on El Roacho Rio: 100 cases of water for his head. Now every shootist, psycho killer, and bad ass is out for the reward.

Meet the Blindman, Nydia, Coffin Jack White, Dog, Blackjack Morgan, Wong Duck, "Cop Warren, Ruby the Dyke, The Shotgun Girls and more. All on a collision course of ultra-violence as they are …The Gunfighters of the Drunken Master

"A relentless story that, at times, makes you beg for mercy. Vivid, nightmarish, subversive and dripping with the vibes of the 42ndStreet aura." - Cory Ulder, writer/director *Incest Death Squad*

"If Sergio Leone and Sam Peckinpah sat down with John Carpenter, this would have been the result" - Todd Sheets, writer/Director *Zombie Bloodbath Trilogy* and *House of Forbidden Secrets*.

"A subversive mind fuck masquerading as a western. Would make a great film." - Gary Kent -writer/director and Stuntman Hall of Famer

"Pete manages to tell an intricate, two fisted, blood soaked adventure tale that screams out to be made as a feature and leaves you wanting more" - Divine Exploitation

Available from Amazon.com or for the signed ,numbered limited edition, contact Pete at fortydeuce@hotmail.com.

WHERFORE ART THOU PASSION?
SO SAYETH: BUBBA THE REDNECK WEREWOLF
(OR FRANKENSTEIN MAKES WOLF MAN)

By Dr. Rhonda Baughman

Introduction

I am tired of you, oh-so clever and constantly never impressed internet carper. A dictionary lists 'carper' as a synonym for reviewer and critic. I only use 'reviewer' and 'critic' if I know your credentials and experience, your skill set and abilities. 'Wathcing and luvving lotsa movies since birtth' is not exactly a credential. It's experience, certainly, misspelled experience—but I need to know you've written something, learned something, attended school or training, created something, or you know, are otherwise in existence on this planet to do something besides make fun of people on the internet and troll comments sections like you're paid to do so.

So, that's why I am here. To defend a work others might readily dismiss as a silly, low-budget time-waster. *Bubba the Redneck Werewolf* is not a waste of time—and in fact, illustrates the opposite: investment. Bubba has a rich and colorful history some may not even be able to grasp initially. Message below from creator Mitch Hyman—and one all of us could stand to listen to. Why? The moral of the story remains that life is too short NOT to engage in your passions to the fullest. If you passion happens to be skulking around the internet, leaving mean notes and messages, take a long, hard look around at why you have no real nor interesting friends to share that lazy passion with.

MESSAGE FROM BUBBA THE REDNECK WEREWOLF CREATOR MITCH HYMAN

Bubba the Redneck Werewolf.

Even if you're not familiar with the name, you'll find yourself wanting to know what this could possibly be. What the comic book world has known and embraced for almost twenty years is now something that others, no matter who, will want to know more about. And time has proven this by giving Bubba one of the oddest histories around.

Bubba has been honored with a satellite launch from NASA which occurred under a full moon and went global via UPI (I have the official NASA photo and documentation showing this), he's been written up with high praise for his originality by a Pulitzer prize winning writer and his paper, The Chicago Tribune. He's been drawn by some of the best known artists in the comic(and some from the film and TV industry) for fans who actually didn't want the usual mainstream characters, but wanted these folks to do their version of Bubba. So, this 24/7 comedic Werewolf (the first in pop culture) has captured many imaginations and sometimes consternation as he is quite the handful to deal with for both myself as his "father" and those who have decided to work with him. But, that's the charm of Bubba and the world he lives in. He's southern as sweet tea and like that beverage he goes along with almost anything you dish up no matter the cuisine's origin.

Bubba is truly an 'All American' concept and hero, but at the same time something the rest of the world can enjoy and appreciate. He represents the 'good guy' in us all. He's inventive, hardworking, altruistic and just trying to keep his life in high gear. He just does it in a manner that simply put is…funny as hell.

Bubba is known in many countries and the comic enjoys a global appeal. We've even had collaborations from people who have never met, worked in different parts of the world, and combined talents to produce published Bubba stories. As Bubba's creator, this proved that Bubba was somewhat iconic. Now the big job ahead, for our production team and actors, was to get that same feeling from off the pages of the comic to the live action screen. And I feel we did just that.

Bubba was conceived in 1994 and has been considered for cartoon shows and movie treatment through most of the time he's been around. There were several attempts to bring him to life but things just didn't work out for more reasons than Bubba has beers in his belly. But in film and TV projects, Bubba was for once, in the 'norm'. Plenty of these types of projects had the same "growing pains". How many versions of 'Spiderman' were there with various creative teams, writers, and directors and so on before we got the one we saw in the early part of this century? Even now, he's been re-launched yet again. That's show biz!

You're now asking why we finally went the independent route? Simple. The final team I was able to put together for the film never wavered from keeping what made the comics so much fun and were able to keep that high energy flowing. They kept Bubba to the heart of what he and his zany friends are. The Bubba comics have a goofy Saturday morning cartoon feel and for the comics that was fine. But film? Well, that really is a whole different animal. We needed to keep the growth in the characters going while keeping the slapstick, verbal gags and just the fun of watching Bubba and his friends fight for the town they love from a threat that is even more supernatural than Bubba himself. Not easy to do. But we all banded together as team and family and pulled it off. I did not do this myself, for sure! Like any multi-faceted child, Bubba needed to be raised by a village. A village of wildly talented people.

We had a team that ranged in age from early twenties to late fifties. This was key to me. This way, we could communicate across the generations and bring a concept and film that almost every generation could enjoy. Add to this, that the people working on this have worked on major motion pictures and television. Some had advised directors like Tim Burton and Steven Spielberg on certain areas of design and others we had on board have helped produce stadium and arena shows for some of the world's biggest live acts. But still, I had many decisions as to how to utilize all this ability to the best degree.

One of those decisions was the production team I picked. This consisted of Caitlyn Foster, our long suffering and cool handed Line Producer, Will Phillips, our esteemed Producer and Assistant Director and, last but far from least, Brendan Rogers, our Director and Producer. These folks are our production partners "And You Films". They have produced plenty of commercials and did a great feature film of their own called, "FLASHBACK". This film was the convincing factor for me in teaming up with them. Their film is a parody of the Hollywood system and has so many pop culture references that it became a drinking game for many of my friends who take a shot when they spot another snarky jibe in the film. If you decide to do this, I suggest you use a designated watcher as you'll be plastered in fifteen minutes or less.

But this is vital! Not the booze, but the understanding of comedy. Bubba is not a horror film, much in that way *Young Frankenstein* or even *Killer Tomatoes* were. Yes, we have some freaky moments and some serious "gore" EFX, but they are not the main focus. What we did here was to take a page out of the big book of Mel Brooks (we actually raise a toast to Mel every time we get together) and then mixed that with the frenetic pacing of a Marx Brothers movie.

Plot and setting are simple: in the town of "Broken Taint" located in Cracker County, FL (the land that time forgot and is damn proud of it!); the local dogcatcher and his fellow townies have been hoping and praying for help in their tiny existences. But instead of reaching more caring and celestial help, they are instead answered and exploited by the Devil himself. It's now up to Bubba and his friends who have been used and cheated by this initially puckish and later malevolent menace to save themselves, their home and their souls from being the start of a plan of global domination. Think of Bubba and friends as guinea pigs being thrown into a Skinner box of obstacles with really no reward unless they band together and gnaw their way to freedom and finish off the cause of their misery. The film, unlike many low budget indie films, does do the most important thing that even major films need to do: a consistent plot and direction while entertaining our audience and getting them to laugh, cheering and worrying along with our characters. And we didn't forget about them booing and hissing the villain, for sure! It is an all-round good time feature length picture that we know people will happily quote and talk about after they view it.

To make this vision of how to give our protagonist and antagonist "looks" that would both amaze and amuse I went to my old friend, Michael Davy. Mike is one of the most inventive and innovative make-up artists around. Mike may not be known to the general public as well as he is known to the icons of the make-up industry though. Mike not only supplies bald caps and other make-up to many motion pictures and television shows, he also is a great inventor. He's created things such as the first cosmetic grade airbrush make-up, foaming gelatin, topical anti-antiperspirant, and more. Mike also has invented something called "Watermelon" which is quickly becoming the replacement for latex due its ability to do the same things latex does, but with neither allergy issues, nor strong adhesives, foundations, and removers. But his inventive side is a matter of genealogy. He is the direct descendent of Sir Humphrey Davy. The same Humphrey Davy who discovered most of the elements in the periodic table and who could claim Mary Shelly as one of his biggest fans. So, yes, we have the great, great, great grandnephew of Frankenstein making the Wolf Man.

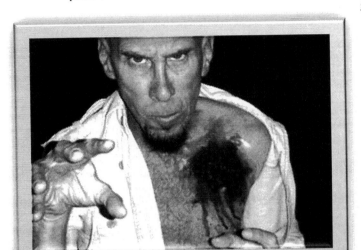

Thanks to Mike we also have the first werewolf in film history that can ... Smile!

He can speak, drink, grin, emote; you name it— and all thanks to Mike's incredible design and sculpting abilities. His design and primary execution of the Devil's make up was pretty impressive, too. When Bubba stepped into the public during filming, people could not differentiate him from not being "real" and wanted to have a drink or just BS with him. The Devil suffered from this amazing style of make-up though...as when he was seen in public, people either threw stuff at him or wanted him to damn and doom them.

And so the line of reality blurs.

Mike was also aided by our Make-Up Key, Karyna Martinez. Karyna began learning certain special techniques from our film's guru of gore, Rick Gonzales, and then moved on to 'one on one' training by Mike for the Bubba character. Karyna also works with a winner of the show 'Face Off' and her ability with silicone and other make-up techniques is astounding. The Devil's make-up needs came from another Gonzales alumni who had also trained at the Joe Blasco School. Then the gore effects and specialty gags involving beheadings, limb loss and the odd bullet shot were performed by blood aficionado J. D. Ellis and the inventive Chris Secosky. Both of whom had been trained on the FX by Rick Gonzales.

But I've saved the best for last...Our actors. Let's face it, these are the people who are going to make all of you out there believe that out there, somewhere, these characters could really exist. These actors were a unique mix. We had polished stage, film and improv folks working alongside of people who had never acted before, but came across as naturals. There was just something about them that made the characters they were going to audition for and later portray really the core of who they were as real human beings. Risky, most would say. But like the most famous long shot bets...this one paid off.

Our Bubba is a great example. Fred Lass was an acquaintance I had known from doing pop culture events like Florida's Spooky Empire show. Fred was the mellow big guy assigned to the security of other stars invited to sign and appear. He also was one of the most naturally funny people I had met in ages. With very little coaching, Fred nailed the Bubba character. Further, I knew myself, as a former DJ and Voice artist that he had that tonal quality I wanted for Bubba. Fred's voice and delivery was a combo of John Goodman channeling Elvis. Being supplied with a brilliantly crafted set of fangs designed and made by Mike Davy, he could speak and be understood almost perfectly. Fred also endured hours and hours in heavy make-up while never losing his grasp on Bubba and as an actor. Fred made Bubba more than real to all of us. To me, he was the embodiment of the way I had always envisioned Bubba could be when he was taken off the comic pages.

The other thing I enjoyed most was to see the more experienced actors sitting and talking with our "newbies" and our director working to get good performances, but all still bonding as friends. We had also a great amount of help from the Cos-Play community. These people know how to bring characters to life and make them real. Thanks to them for showing up at 3am, putting their lives and jobs on hold to help us pull this off. Add to this the locations we used and the fact the people who owned or managed them not only welcomed us, but looked forward to our coming back and then even fed us and watched over us—a beautiful group of people all around.

Now speaking of the more experienced actors…Our Bobbi-Jo is an up and coming actress who the world will be seeing more of in the near future and we are happy and lucky as hell to have her before she becomes someone way out of my meager price range. Her name is Malone Thomas and she brought real dimension to the role of Bubba's girlfriend. Then there's the character of Drunk Cletus, a Vietnam Vet who lost his most prized possessions in the war and when he goes on—sometimes endlessly about it and the war—you begin to want to hear him continue the diatribe and you'll, like most of us, find yourself quoting him after seeing his portrayal by Gary Norris, a vet himself of many theater productions. Sara Humbert, another well-seasoned actor who plays Bartender 'Jaimie Sue' could throw lines and expressions that could heat up a polar bear in December and then cool off the equator in August. Hyperbole, you say? Well-deserved, I counter! Also, watch for our other experienced member of the bar and I don't mean he's an attorney: Bill Dabney is his name and he adds a special spice to the brew. Then our human Bubba, Chris Crown, did a great job of establishing the loser and knucklehead persona of the pre-Wolf Bubba. Electrically frenzied is the only phrase for Chris—he was like watching a controlled tornado of comedy. Biker Bob, our Master of the 'Two Stroke Discipline' was played to perfection by Dan Bedell.

Thanks to Brendan Rogers, we acquired the services of Production Designer, Joseph Stone. Joe has worked on tons of films for the major market and as an armorer (weapons specialist) for them as well. What he did to make our bar and Bubba's trailer is something that makes this film worth watching just by itself. It looked like the Joker and Freddy Krueger had teamed up to become survivalists from hell.

And there were many others who helped on this production that it would take two articles to tell of them all. If you go to our IMDB or Bubba Facebook page, you'll see them all.

Was everything perfect on set? Of course not. Did we have problems? Tons. Did we bring you a great film and fun experience? Well, we think so but that's really up to viewers to determine. We can't ask more than that from all of you out there.

So, we plan to see you all soon the movies.

THE PRINCE OF DARKNESS: KEVIN SULLIVAN

I discovered pro wrestling in the mid 70's. Living in the New York area, we had the World Wide Wrestling Federation, WWWF. They ran monthly at Madison square Garden in NYC. The Champion was Bruno Sanmartino who was the biggest draw wrestling had at that time period. Bruno on the card = sellout. The undercard featured guys like Domenic DeNucci, Tony Garea, Dean Ho, Irish Pat Barrett, The Blackjacks, Gorilla Monsoon, Ivan Koloff and others. Kevin Sullivan entered the WWWF at this time as a "baby face".

Sullivan was a short guy who would get over on "jobbers" like Frankie Williams, Jose Estrada, Artie Palmer and others on TV. He would battle mid card "heels" like Johnny Rodz, Baron Sicluna, Tony Altimore, and others. Then would lose to main event guys. Back then, you never got a main event on TV. You had to pay for that. TV was geared to get you emotionally involved, and, by doing that, you would pay to see shows at MSG and other venues. WWWF had what I would call a "plodding" style of wrestling. Hit, punch, kick and stomp the foot for effect. Punches were visibly pulled, but it was all we had. Then I found this station on UHF.

Remember no cable or internet back then. I was playing with my antenna and turned to channel 47 at 11pm. It was a Spanish station. There was some sort of wrestling from Florida of all places. I caught the last ten minutes of the show that ended in a violent draw. I made note of the time and the channel. Next week I tuned in. This wasn't the wrestling I had seen up north. This was some violent stuff. This show ended with some guy bleeding. I had never seen this before. Blood was banned in the North East, so were masked wrestlers and, at MSG, there was an 11pm curfew. Now I was hooked, I saw guys I had read about in wrestling magazines. The Brisco Brothers, Dusty Rhodes, King Curtis, Jos LeDuc, Greg Valentine, Bugsy McGraw, and Frank "the Hammer" Goodish before Vince McMahon SR gave him the name Bruiser Brody.

Other guys were Bob Orton JR, Mike Graham, Steve Keirn, Bob Roop, Dick Slater, and Terry Funk. During this time, Sullivan was learning the business. He learned from Vince SR. Vince had everything set up for six months in advance as he handpicked Bruno's challengers. Kevin toured the territories in the south, went to San Francisco, then to Georgia where he turned heel on Tony Atlas and Steve Keirn. Kevin went to Florida and became fast friends with Mike Graham, son of promoter Eddie Graham. Eddie was considered one of the best minds in the business and took Kevin under his wing.

What I didn't know was that the WWWF had a deal with Graham. They aired the show on 47 so fans would want to see the Florida wrestlers. Eddie would send guys up north to work an MSG show. Trouble was they would adapt to that "plodding" style. Wrestlers wanted to work for Eddie, especially guys who hated the harsh winters of other territories. Eddie ran different towns every night, but every Sunday the big show was at The Eddie Graham Sportatorium. The place was packed every Sunday night. JJ Dillon told me that one of the largest rattlesnake dens in the state was behind the building. First guy in had the job of checking for the snakes. The building was a huge, steel barn.

Eddie would book the shows with a solid hard hitting main event, or a bloodbath. Specialty matches like chain matches, cage matches, first blood matches, Texas Death matches, and loser leaves town matches were common. We never got these in the north east, maybe a cage match now and then, but never this stuff. If you think that ECW was an original idea, think again. Paul Heyman worked in Florida, so where do you think he got some of his ideas? Eddie is still considered one of the best finish men in the business.

Sullivan turned heel in the 80's. I forget exactly what happened, but they did something that was completely ahead of its time, a wrestling video. Sullivan was on a beach under a full moon in November. He was going to summon one of his minions from the sea, The Purple Haze. The waters broke and a strange, yet buff figure came out of the sea, The Purple Haze. It was a stunning visual which blew the viewer's mind. The Purple Haze was wrestler Mark Lewin. Lewin started wrestling in 1953 and was a matinee idol with his tag team partner, Don Curtis. Lewin was making more money than pro ball players at the time.

Lewin changed his persona in 1963 to 'Maniac "Mark Lewin. He would vacillate between heel and face for most of his career. He spent the late '60s and early '70s wrestling in Australia, New Zealand and Singapore. He married a Polynesian Princess. Sullivan, at that time, did several tours over there and had met Lewin. Sullivan also learned things there that he added to his gimmick. Sullivan was called a Satanist and a devil worshipper, but at no time did he ever actually say that he was. He used the word "Abudiune" which is a Hindu god. Too the overly religious southern rednecks, this was a devil worshipper. Sullivan would paint his face, carve a Mansonesque "X" on his forehead, mutter jiberish, and wear black robes.

Lewin told Sullivan that for this gimmick to work, they had to live it 24/7. Lewin never went out of character. He and Sullivan showed up and left wearing their robes. When they went to eat, Lewin never spoke and Sullivan ordered for him. Sullivan's big feuds would be against Dusty Rhodes, Barry Windham, Blackjack Mulligan and anyone allied with them. Blackjack had been feuding with Andre the Giant in the WWWF and left for Florida to help his son, Barry Windham. Windham was one of the hottest stars in the Florida territory. Sullivan had to add to his stable so he took Bob Roop, a solid wrestler who had worked Florida, but was sort of old news. Roop shaved half of his head and face. He painted the shaved half and became Maka Singh. Sullivan's girlfriend and future wife, Nancy, became the fallen angel complete with bondage gear and real pythons.

Sullivan would go nuts on the air, especially during interviews. Lewin would stand in the background drooling. Sullivan would beat the shit out of a jobber, then call in his "minions" to finish him off. Sullivan would attack Dusty and leave him bleeding. Once he used a broken beer bottle to slice up Blackjack on camera. Sullivan feuded with Blackjack for over a year. Sullivan called Blackjack the most unselfish guy he ever worked with. Blackjack was close to seven feet tall, Sullivan was 5'9" and Sullivan was beating the crap out of him every night, usually with the help of his crew. Sullivan told him, "Jack, you have to get heat on me" aka beat me. BJ told him that they should keep playing it out.

Truth be told, Blackjack was a guy with a history of a bad temper. Fuck with him, piss him off and you got your as kicked for real. Being a true professional here, he knew that the day he actually beat Sullivan clean would end the feud and also the $$$ it was drawing. Sullivan was going to bring someone new into his group. Luna Vachon was the daughter of Paul "Butcher "Vachon, from the legendary Vachon wrestling family which included Maurice " Mad Dog " Vachon and Vivian Vachon. Luna's cover was that she was a reporter, Trudy Herd, looking for a story. The angle was that Sullivan would knock her out on camera.

Sullivan admitted that he was loath to actually hit a woman. Luna kept prodding him "not to hold back" that she was a Vachon and could take it. Sullivan really had no intention of decking her until the moment arrived and she walked past him and said 'lay it in and don't be a pussy about it.' A tad pissed, Sullivan really nailed her prompting the fans that were there every week to really turn on him. After that, Luna had half her head shaved, the start of her trade mark Mohawk, went nuts and joined Sullivan's group. Luna teamed with The Lock (Winnona Littleheart) and became The Daughters of Darkness Tag team.

An interesting situation occurred when the tag team of The Road Warriors came to Florida for a week. The Road Warriors were huge at the time and were in demand all over the world. Problem was that they had no intention of putting over (letting win) any of their opponents. Sullivan told them that may be the deal, but I have to live with Blackjack after you guys leave. So they set it up that every match ended with a DQ, a count out, or a run in. I was in Florida at this time on vacation. The main event at The Eddie Graham Sportatorium was the Road Warriors with Precious Paul Ellering vs. Sullivan and Maka Singh. Blackjack vs. The Purple Haze was the co-main event.

Sullivan and Singh were first out, then the Road Warriors came out and the roof blew off the place. The two teams beat the shit out of each other. Then The Purple Haze attacked Precious Paul at ringside. That act brought out Blackjack after The Haze. The brawl spilled out of the ring and outside into the parking lot. The same show, with a few variations, went from town to town all week. I lost that UHF station as Vince JR had taken over and was gobbling up talent. Sullivan tried taking his gimmick to Jim Crocket Promotions in the Carolinas, but it had to be way toned down as the Crocket Family was very religious. Sullivan would take Lewin and Roop to Hawaii for Polynesian Pacific Wrestling were they feuded with Lars Anderson (Larry Heiniemi) who was the Champ/booker.

Sullivan spent 1987 to 1992 with WCW were he was the head of several "heel" factions. The Varsity Club with Mike Rotunda, Rick Steiner, and Steve 'Doctor Death" Williams. Then the short lived Sullivan's Slaughterhouse with Buzz Sawyer and Cactus Jack. After his contract expired, he went to

Japan for FMW (Frontier Martial Arts Wrestling) were he hooked up with Ed Farhat (The Original Shiek) and battled Atsushi Onita in several blood baths. He then joined Victor Quionies Wing Promotion.

Sullivan then went to Jim Cornette's Smokey Mountain Wrestling were he had feuds with Brian Lee and Ronnie Garvin. Then he was in ECW for about a year, teaming with The Tasmaniac (Tazz) and reteaming with Cactus Jack. Sullivan was still in WCW in '94. So was Cactus Jack. Jack had earned the ire of then booker, Ric Flair, when he spit on the WCW Tag Belt while cutting a promo on ECW TV. Cactus Jack's WCW contract was almost up. He knew that if he stayed, he'd get buried by Flair. So he fought Sullivan in a 'Loser leaves WCW" match and went to ECW full time.

Sullivan created The Dungeon of doom to take out Hulk Hogan, who had just signed with WCW. Sullivan was now The Taskmaster. His stable include The Butcher (ake Ed Leslie or Brutus Beefcake), Meng, Loch Ness (The Giant Haystacks from Great Britain), Kamala, The Barbarian, The Yeti, One Man Gang, Big Bubba Rogers, and the Giant (Big Show). Problem was that Hogan was getting booed. Sullivan told Hogan that he had to turn heel, it was time. Hogan didn't want to and neither did his "advisors". Sullivan convinced Hogan that it was the way to go. He said " look, you're getting booed at every show." Sullivan kept Hogan at his house until the night of the big turn so none of his advisors could talk him out of it. "Hollywood" Hogan became his new persona.

Sullivan had an apparent dislike for Horseman Brian Pillman. Pillman was the "loose cannon" as he wasn't under contract and showed up in ECW. Pillman had a "respect" match with Sullivan. Halfway into the match, Pillman bailed. He grabbed the mike and said "I respect you, booker man". a cheap shot as Sullivan was the booker. Pillman left the building, and screwed WCW by joining the WWE. Horseman, Arn Anderson had to finish the match with Sullivan. Sullivan started a similar feud with Horseman Chris Benoit. The angle was that Benoit stole Woman (Nancy Sullivan) from Kevin. Nancy took the name "Woman" when she managed the tag team of Doom (Ron Simmons and Butch Reed) in WCW. Trouble was Nancy and Kevin were having problems and she left him for Benoit. Sullivan and Benoit beat the living shit out of each other as they both worked stiff. Sullivan lost a retirement match to Benoit.

Reason for this was the entire booking team was fired and Sullivan was made head booker. This really pissed off some of the locker room. Benoit, Eddie Guerrero, Dean Malenko, and Perry Saturn would quit the night after and join the WWE. Sullivan was fired before WCW was sold in 2001. In 2007 Chris Benoit killed Nancy, then his son, Daniel before committing suicide in one of the biggest tragedies in the history of wrestling. Sullivan would bounce around the country, working for various promotions. He also opened a gym in Key West. He appeared as a legend for National Wrestling Superstars several times in NJ. He showed up under a mask at one of the Extreme Reunion shows. He is semi-retired and living on an island off the coast of Washington state.

Blackjack Mulligan went back to the WWE. He had an interview segment called Blakjack's Barbecue. He was supposed to feud with Cowboy Ron Bass, but got pissed off at a remark made to him by Pat Patterson and left. He retired in 1988.

Mark Lewin went to World Class Championship Wrestling in Texas as part of Playboy Gary Hart's stable with Killer Brooks and the One Man Gang. He retired in 1998.

Barry Windham went on to do great things in the WWE, WCW, and other promotions. He became a producer for the WWE in 2007 and was let go in 2008. He suffered a heart attack on Oct 26, 2011. He recovered and was inducted into the WWE Hall of Fame in 2012.

Luna Vachon wrestled all over the world and had several runs in the WWE. She showed up in ECW and tagged with Tommy Dreamer against Raven and Stevie Richards. She married wrestler Dave Heath (the Vampire Warrior). She was instrumental in the success of Woman's Superstars Uncensored where her altercation with The Diva Killaz put WSU on the map. She teamed with my friend Pryme Tyme Amy Lee as Satan's Sisters. Sadly she died in 2010 at age 48 from an overdose of pain killers.

Boop Roop retired in 1988 after injuring his neck in a car accident. He did a cameo in Stallone's wrestling movie, Paradise Alley.

Dusty Rhodes still works for the WWE behind the scenes and his two sons, Dustin and Cody compete there.

THE ROAD TO INSANITY
A GUIDE TO THE DEATHMATCH
By Mr. Insanity Toby Cline

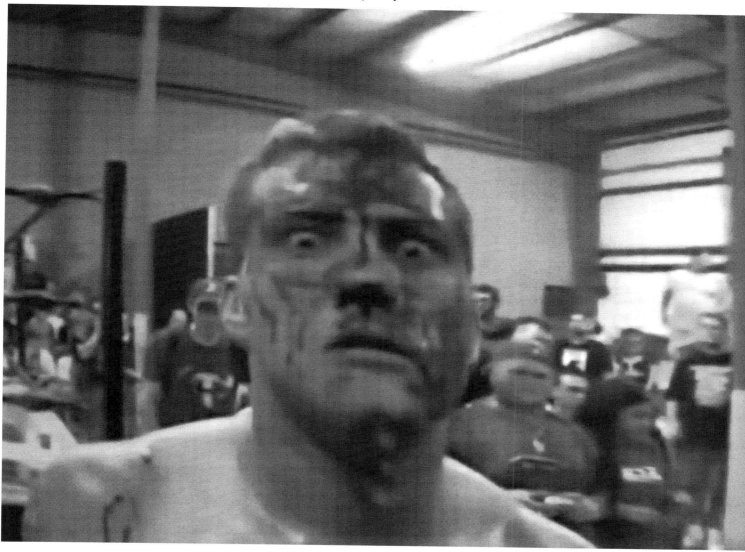

I never intended to be a "deathmatch "worker!!. It all started innocently enough: a college dropout walks into a wrestling school, following his lifelong dream of becoming a pro wrestler. Growing up a Hulk A Maniac gave me the fantasy of being a rich and famous WWE Superstar. You find out very quickly in this business that very few get famous and almost nobody gets rich. So what's the trick in gaining notoriety? What the secret to getting more than a tank of gas out of greedy promoters?

For a small town Ohio boy, the answer came in a ring full of broken glass, thumb tacks and barbed wire. My first "deathmatch" was against Hardcore Legend Mad Man Pondo in 1998 at a fairgrounds show for Pizza Joe's Championship Wrestling. I instantly loved the crowd reaction when weapons were used. Some people were out there putting on wrestling clinics and were truly gifted athletes, but the crowd sat quietly on their hands. Then I get blasted in the face with a stop sign, blood spews from my face and the place goes nuts.

I should mention that I was trained in the art of pro wrestling first and foremost. I was traveling the Indy Circuit for almost two years, getting gas money to travel to places like Steel City Wrestling in Pittsburg, Cleveland All Pro Wrestling, American States Wrestling Alliance, House of Pain Wrestling in

Rochester New York, and countless other spot shows here and there. But I would return home broke and frustrated. And then the Deathmatch changed all that.

After that first deathmatch with Pondo, and the payday for doing it, it sparked my interest for sure. Shortly after, I was booked on a show with Ian Rotten, and things were about to really take off. Ian Rotten booked me for IWA Mid-South King of the Death Matches 2000. This was the first of many Deathmatch tournaments I would participate in over the next ten years. Matches included The 200 light tubes Deathmatch, The Caribbean Spiderweb, Unlucky 13 Staple Gun, Fans Bring the Weapons, Log cabin Light Tubes, Barefoot Thumbtack, Pool of Lobsters, and many more that you would have to see to believe. Although I'd leave the building bloody ad sore, my adrenaline would be pumping and the paydays received would be equal to a week's pay at a regular job. A ten minute Deathmatch would pay me at least $500 or more.

During the 2000's, I worked plenty of regular wrestling matches, but I was definitely becoming stereotyped as a Deathmatch worker. This was fine for a little longer.

Three factors launched my Deathmatch career to the next level: my friendship with Pondo, Mike Burns and smart Mark Video, and my matches with Necro Butcher. Mike burns began booking the Deathmatches for Philly's Combat Zone Wrestling. He was the owner of Smart Mark Video and had filmed dozens of my matches in numerous promotions. So here I was debuting against notorious bank robber, Nick Gage in the first CZW Tournament of Death. That was the start of a seven year run in CZW, where I would go on to be a two time Iron Man Champion and a one-time Tag team champion with Necro Butcher. I loved the Philadelphia crowds, the zany matches and loved being flown out of an airport to go to work! I ended up doing the annual Tournament of Death six different times and the annual Cage of Death three years in a row.

Ian Rotten was the first to book me in a feud with the Necro Butcher for IWA Mid-south. Necro was starting to get a bad reputation for beating people up. Ian thought our styles would work together in a match and the fans agreed. I first worked him in 2002 for the IWA, and the feud would continue from coast to coast for the next eight years. I rank our IWA King of the Death Matches 2003 and 2004 as out two standout matches. And after beating each other up over and over, all the light tubes busted, chair shots, and STIFF punches, we decided it would be healthier to team together more often than fight each other. We formed a tag team, The Tough Crazy Bastards, and it went over with the promoters and the fans huge. Altogether, Necro and I would face each other or team up in six different IWA King of the Death Match tournaments. I would go on to win the 2005 King of the Death Matches by defeating Necro in the finals.

My friendship with Mad Man Pondo would open up a very unique door in late 2005. The world of Big Japan Pro Wrestling and Deathmatch wrestling was huge in Japan. I would go on to do three successful tours with BJP. I would wrestle in insane matches with the likes of Masada, Crazy Monkey Jun Kasi, Shadow WX, Ito, Badboy Hido, Pondo and 2 Tuff Tony. I loved the Japanese culture and the respect of the fans. I did the 2005 and 2006 tours over there, made some good money, and met some good people.

By the end of 2006, my story began to take a turn for the worse. I was getting booked constantly in death matches from coast to coast. I was getting burnt out of the hardcore wrestling scene, and I began abusing prescription pain pills daily to even compete in the matches. Addiction runs rampant in death match wrestling, and in the late 2000s, overdoses and suicide began to become normal occurrences among the workers. I will gladly get into that another day for anyone who is interested.

There were plenty of ups and downs in the twelve years I competed in the Deathmatch. From the highs of competing overseas and making some quick cash, to the lows of becoming an opiate addict. Then getting numerous phone calls in the middle of the night that another close friend had died. It was an eventful and bumpy trip.

Altogether, I worked in dozens of Death Matches. Numerous IWA king of the Death Matches and CZW Tournament of Death, winning the 2005 King of the Death Matches and 2009 Hatchet Wrestling's Brink of Death 3. I worked for the Japanese Yazuka, The Insane Clown Posse, scumbag promoters, money marks, and everybody else running these tournaments from coast to coast. To quote the late Hunter S Thompson "I bought the ticket, and then I took the ride.

[*Publisher's note: Mr Insanity, Toby Klein, did indeed take the ride. I met Toby at Cinema Wasteland a few years ago. We became friends and Toby wanted to do a Death Match show in conjunction with Cinema Wasteland. I took him to the Cuyahoga County fair Grounds where he made a deal to rent a building and put on Night of the Living Death Matches, six matches with horror film themes. One of the wrestlers involved turned this in to the State Athletic Commission and we were told we would be fined heavily if any blood was spilled.*

Toby then addressed the fact that he has a problem with pain killers and checked into rehab. Today he is clean, raising his family, and wrestling part time for a couple of local promoters. He and myself co-host my Cinema

Wasteland Hardcore Wrestling Hour which has become a must attend event on Saturday morning.]

CUMMING SOON
By Josh Hadley

An oft overlooked area of the Grindhouse is the pubic area... porn. Real porn came from the grindhouse. *The Devil In Miss Jones, The Jade Pussycat, Cafe Flesh, Nightdreams, Forced Entry, Pleasure Palace, Behind The Green Door, Pussy Talk* and *The Satisfiers Of Alpha Blue*. Directors such as Rinse Dream, Gerard Damiano, Bob Chin and the Mitchell Brothers. These are the forgotten films of the Grindhouse era... the fuck films.

When people think of film (as an artform) they rarely allow for the very idea that adult/porn/porno/XXX could be at the same as any "real" movie... least of all a real Grindhouse movie. X matters and has influenced far more than many would like to credit it with. Lars von Trier says that his film sycophantic ego masturbation film Nymphomaniac (with full on hardcore scenes) is not porno but instead it is art... which leads to the only way that can be interpenetrated as being that porn cannot be art according to Trier. Fucking self-indulgent auto-fellating shithead.

To many of you X is nothing more than cheap prurient exhibitionism meant to titillate and nothing more... to stimulate something other than the mind (such as the prostate or the suppressed gag reflex). The Godfather of Adult, Bill Margold, takes issue with the use of the term X to describe these films "I think that X-Rated term was whored out and overused. Back in the day, I would have preferred Explicitly Adult instead of tossing X's around Ju-Ju-Bees. Although squandered in the minds of fools who think that by putting an X on something it gives them a license to degrade humanity and insult their viewers with repellant images, the 24th letter of the alphabet is a cornerstone for Freedom of Expression and must be utilized carefully...and wisely."

X and it's Grindhouse placement matter for a variety of reasons not the least of which is that many of the freedoms allowed in "mainstream" films only happened due to the efforts made by the 'pornographers'. All of the taboos in film were first broken not in an MPAA approved film but in an adult film, one showing in a theater with sticky floors and equally sticky seats. With porno being a (relatively) underground medium they were allowed to get away with more in their films, both in terms of actual content and of the freedom in HOW the films were made. With no studios to make marketing decisions and with having a market of presold audiences the filmmakers were able to be creative and do things a studio film would never have allowed. Race mixing, bloodletting, acts of deviation, brutal satire etc... The story of a movie such as *Behind the Green Door* simply could not have been made in any other environment besides that of a 1972 independent adult films. Coupled with the films nascent story being that of pseudo-rape or at the very least a rape fantasy played out before an audience (in movie) this was the unique filmmaking techniques the Mitchell brothers employed including that of a seven minute long slow motion (color) strobing cumshot set to booming music... this was not the kind of filmmaking that no movie studio would have allowed in a film at this time. This was the true freedom of an unencumbered id run amok and I believe a symbol of the reason that X matters.

Filmmakers such as Stephen Sayadian took the idea of art within X to levels undreamed of with his almost hallucinatory trips into the inner mind that we dare not touch. A picture such as *Nightdreams* is the very definition of an art film on every level and it alone set a standard that remained untouched in the adult world let alone the "mainstream" world. Prior to *Nightdreams* though Sayadian made *Cafe Flesh*, an adult film that set a new standard in both its storytelling and in the hardcore aspects. Along with *Caligula*, *Cafe Flesh* was one of the only hardcore films to be reedited and re-released in "R" rated versions to mass audiences. The funny thing about both *Caligula* and *Cafe Flesh* was that the hardcore scenes in both films were not meant to be alluring nor to turn you on, in fact the hardcore scenes in *Cafe Flesh* are so intentionally un-erotic they are almost challenging you to get hard watching them… almost daring you to find this as eroticism and yet many Grindhouse patrons were indeed aroused which honestly says more about them than the film.

This shocking and savage attack on the very sensibilities of the libido itself is something that mainstream Hollywood would not understand for decades to come; actually giving the audience a challenge. X once meant walking away with a feeling of having been enlightened as well as a feeling of being sticky. The artists of the Grindhouse fuck film have proven again and again that being a hardcore adult film does not mean you stop being an artist.

There was even a time when hardcore porns moved out of the Grindhouse and played to mass middle class and upper class audiences right out in the open… the era of Porno Chic. Porno Chic was a time when celluloid scintillation was at the corner theater and middle class couples would go out to the movies for *Deep Throat* or *The Devil in Miss Jones* over *The Godfather* or *American Graffiti* with no stigma of these being "dirty" movies… these were movies the same as any other. 42nd Street had come of age… (cum of age as it were). Porno Chic was a fairly short lived period but Porno Chic was a nationwide phenomenon which alone proves that X made an impact on film and yet is very quickly forgotten by those who wish to dismiss porn as nothing more than base urges and scandalous sexcapades. What is the (real) difference though between a movie such as *The Satisfiers of Alpha Blue* or *Sex Crimes 2084* and *American Pie* or *The Hangover*? Why is it that a film like *Sex Crimes 2084* which posits the message that sex without attachment is meaningless, is disregarded as salacious while a film about

teens that will have sex with anything they encounter is hailed by critics? This is a matter of not just semantics but a matter of perception; the comprehension that adult films (and all Grindhouse cinema) are also art is one that is sorely lacking today and yet there is more awareness today of this fact than ever before which says more about how far we have come and less about the medium itself.

X has taken a huge hit in quality in the last 2 decades and has simply became what it was always (erroneously) believed to be... a collection of scenes that are loosely connected by the threadbare of a "story". Go and watch one of the Grindhouse era porns... they had more story elements than orifice penetrations and they had good stories at that... the kind where you kept watching after you finished all over yourself. You wanted to see what happened next.

The question then is why the ignominy of X and the pride of NC-17? Why does the movie *Kids* get critical accolades for its "real" portrayal of sex while *Sex World* is tossed aside with its heartfelt and intensely true depiction of alienation and the breakdown of relationships? You were always taught from a young age that sex films which showed penetration were bad for you all the while you were given the okay to like sex films where women were mere objects to be lusted over. *Porky's* is okay but *Cabaret Sin* will melt your soul and crush your spirit. There is a massive campaign to keep X films underground by the very people who indulge in these films as they are ashamed of themselves and a way to deflect that shame is to project it.

Hell, the list of porno actors and actresses that later went onto mainstream film acceptance is staggering and yet adult is still seen as that world beneath that of even exploitation films and yet these worlds tended to cross even more frequently.

Sonny Landham from *48 Hours* and *Predator* started out as a stud in adult films. Sylvester Stallone was the titular Stud in *The Party at Kitty and Stud's* (aka *Italian Stallion*). Jean Claude Van Damme famously did a few gay jerk off movies before his 'real' career took off. Jackie Chan and Cameron Diaz took whatever work was available to them at the time and that was porn. Technically the entire cast of *Caligula* all did porn but that was later in most of their careers. Robert Kerman danced between many worlds, he would do a porn one week, then appear in an exploitation film such as *Cannibal Holocaust*, do another adult film and then pop up on *Hill Street Blues* and even in 2002 had a small role in Sam Raimi's *Spider-Man*. Michelle Bauer started out as a background actor in *Nightdreams,* moved up to lead actress in *Cafe Flesh* and *Bad Girls* and yet she claims her first REAL film was The Tomb in 1986... all of those other movies were just adult so they didn't count I guess. Luis De Jesus (Ralphus from *Blood Sucking Freaks*) freely moved between the worlds of exploitation films and adult in a way that few have ever been able to sustain. What I find the most disturbing about all of this is that not a single one of the "A-List" actors that did these X movies is proud of them, they try to ignore them and hope that people forget they ever did these or in more cases than not they attempted to sue and/or halt the companies from releasing them. Really Stallone, you are embarrassed by *Italian Stallion* but not *Rhinestone Cowboy*?

Many times the crews of "mainstream" films would moonlight on adult sets in between studio work... hey work is work right? Usually due to guild rules or simply out of embarrassment and shame they would work under pseudonyms which makes for cataloging all of these more than a little frustrating. For instance famed cinematographer Gary Graver worked with Orson Welles for the last 25 years of Welles career... and also would shoot porns under the name Robert McCallum. Many cameramen, boom ops, sound engineers and even writers would supplement their incomes from the adult world. Abel Ferrera started out directing adult movies and went from *9 Lives of a Wet Pussy* to Grindhouse classics such as *Ms. 45* and *Bad Lieutenant* as well as episodes of *Miami Vice*. Gregory Dark started out directing adult standbys such as *New Wave Hookers, The Devil in Miss Jones 3 & 4* (cough) and the *Between the Cheeks* series moving on to directing music videos for Britney Spears, Onyx, and Bone Thugs-N-Harmony. Jerry Stahl got his start writing the films of Rinse Dream and then went "mainstream" going from *Nightdreams* and *Cafe Flesh* to *Moonlighting, Alf, Twin Peaks,* and *CSI* along with the Michael Bay film *Bad Boys II*. Francis Delia started out directing for Rinse Dream as well and moved onto network TV with Michael Mann's *Crime Story, Max Headroom, Friday The 13th The Series, War Of The Worlds The Series* and music videos by Weird Al and Wall Of Voodoo.

It seems that it is frighteningly difficult to keep balancing the worlds of X and the "mainstream" as the stigma of X still lingers but my question is why is it still like this? Why does having Hustler on my resume HURT my chances when attempting to sell something to Rolling Stone or Wired? Why is there still a stigma from X moving as an undercurrent through the "mainstream" world and why most of all does X still impede acceptance into the "big leagues"? Adult films are still films and those who work in adult are just as talented and creative as those who work for Warner Brothers or Universal and in a strange way they are better people because they are not deluding themselves into thinking they something they are not, they are the only honest people in the field, no pretension that they are making REAL movies as Michelle Bauer illustrates with her discounting her adult work as not being REAL movies.

Grindhouse fuck flicks are something to be admired as much for their sex as for their audacious ability to stimulate multiple organs simultaneously.

CHESTY MORGAN: AN IMPERFECT PAIR
by Douglas Waltz

Born in 1937 as Liliana Wilczkowska, Chesty Morgan had two things going for her. Both of them were her boobs. With a chest measurement of 73 inches that were completely natural, she knew the one way to make some serious cash.

Exotic Dancing.

She started in the 70s and worked until 1991, a pretty lengthy career for any dancer. She appeared in four films, but was cut out of two of them. Her entire film legacy was a pair of features from the legendary Doris Wishman. Wishman knew what she was working with and created a pair of legendary exploitation films the likes of which we would never see again.

An epic pair of movies about an epic pair.

Classic!

DEADLY WEAPONS

1974

Produced and Directed by Doris Wishman

Story by Judy J. Kushner (as J.J. Kushner)

Starring Chesty Morgan (as Zsa Zsa) Harry Reems, Greg Reynolds, Saul Meth, Phillips Stahl, Mitchell Fredericks, Denis Purcell and John McMohon

Make-Up Saul and Miriam Meth

Edited by Lou Burdi

Director of Photography Juan Fernandez

So, these three toughs break into an apartment looking for something. While Larry (Greg Reynolds) is rifling through the guys' stuff Tony (Harry Reems) and another tough beat the crap out of the guy. Larry finds a little booklet and pockets it and tells the other toughs he found nothing.

Larry wastes no time using the information and calls a guy by the name of Mr. Panty and tries to blackmail him. Then he goes to the bedroom where Crystal is sleeping. They make love. Later, Larry goes for a walk while Crystal gets cleaned up and takes a nice, long bath. Larry comes back from his walk and seeing that Crystal is still bathing goes back to the phone and tells Mr. Panty that he has two days to turn over $100,000. Mr. Panty threatens to go to the police, but Larry knows that he won't.

Larry and Crystal are having coffee when he tells her he has to go out of town for a little while and gives her the little book of information for safekeeping. She isn't happy about it, but she understands.

Larry meets up with Tony and they talk to the boss who we never see, but he has a nasty scar on his hand. He tells him they need to get that book back at any cost. Larry never lets on that he has the goods.

Crystal goes to visit her father and they have an argument about Larry and she leaves.

Meanwhile Tony and another tough corner a guy at gunpoint in a stairwell. He tries to get away and they beat him up trying to force him to tell them where the info is. He tells them nothing. Tony produces a dagger, stabs the guy and then wipes his prints off of the blade leaving it on the corpse. When Tony calls in to report that it was a wash he tells the boss that they need to get Larry. When he gets the go ahead he calls one of his cohorts to tell him that they are on the job. Tony's woman, Eve (Denise Purcell) hears the entire conversation.

Larry calls Crystal to tell her that they can get married. The call is interrupted when Tony and his partner, nicknamed Captain Hook because he has an eyepatch. Hook shoots Larry dead and they are unaware that Crystal is still on the phone.

She hears their travel plans as Tony hands Hook a ticket to Vegas and tells him the name of the hotel he will be staying at. Tony mentions that he will be going to Miami while things cool down. When Tony gets back to his place to pack, Eve is waiting with a drink in hand. Tony has one and then starts packing. She asks to go with him and he refuses. She convinces him to make love to her.

Meanwhile, Crystal is staring out the window of her house and remembering the good times with Larry. She tries to sleep later, but she can't. She decides that the only course of action will be revenge.

Since she knows where Captain Hook is staying she heads for Vegas first. Unfortunately, without his real name she has very little to go on. This does not stop her from calling the front desk a couple of times asking for Captain Hook which is pretty funny. She decides to bait the hook by answering an ad for burlesque dancers. When she marches into the office, the manager has his head buried in a paper and asks if she has any experience. When she says no he tells her to beat it. She takes her shirt off and asks again. He looks up and hires her on the spot.

Then we are treated to a terrible dance number that would shame any true burlesque dancer, but we know that her dancing isn't what got her the job. She strips down pretty quick and when she does the reveal of her 73s the number is over. They used stock footage for the audience and I'm not sure where they got it, but there are kids in the audience. Apparently it is true what they say: What happens in Vegas stays in Vegas.

Later, the boss hits on her and she tells him she is not interested and runs off. He catches up to her and pours it on nice and thick and she still refuses his advances. He tells her she is finished and to do her last set before leaving.

As luck would have it, Hook is in the audience and he is mesmerized by Crystal. When she sees the eyepatch she puts two and two together and comes up with Captain Hook. She goes with him back to his place and explains she will be meeting Tony later and asks if he knows where he will be. Hook is happy to give her the info and offers to make drinks. She spikes Hook's drink and it knocks him down and out. Crystal uses her massive breasts to smother Hook to death.

Her mission accomplished she is on the first plane to Miami to track down Tony. With the information she got from Hook that is pretty easy and she approaches him while he is catching some sun poolside. She tries to make small talk and Tony could care less. He walks off.

A little while later, Tony and Eve are all dressed up and headed to the bar. It's pretty obvious that this is just someone's bar in their basement, but it works. They order drinks and then Crystal shows up and starts pestering Tony enough that Eve gets angry and storms off thinking that Tony is having a fling with Crystal. Tony chases after her and they fight and she walks out of the room. Tony chases her to the elevator and convinces her to come back so they can kiss and make up. While they are making out Even tells Tony that she heard his conversation with the boss about killing Larry. Larry responds by taking off his tie and strangling her to death with it. He walks into another room and Crystal is on the bed waiting for him. He starts making out with her and then says he has to go. She offers him a drug laced drink and he downs it. Paralyzed by the drug he is helpless while Crystal also smothers him to death. It is interesting to note in both cases that before she kills she raises her arms way over her head in some kind of bizarre pose. It reminded me of an insect attacking its prey. I don't know if that was intentional or just something they did to make her boobs stick out better. I thought it lent a creepy/cool vibe to the scene.

With her revenge complete she goes home, stopping to visit her father to tell him she is going to turn herself in and give up the little book that Larry entrusted to her. That night she is awakened by a noise. When she goes to investigate she finds the man with the scar rifling through her things. And, it's her father. She goes to call the police, confident that he won't shoot her. He shoots her and then goes over to a set of drawers to look for the book. He sets the gun down and Crystal gets the gun and shoots him. She slowly crawls over to his dead body, lays her head on his chest and dies.

Deadly Weapons exists for one reason. Chesty Morgan. Her all natural pair of 73s make her more of an oddity than anything else. She seems like a nice girl and while her acing is wooden I did like the concept of death by breasts. Breasts are supposed to be life giving and she is using a monstrous version of them to kill instead. Pretty deep stuff for a Doris Wishman movie. So, while she does disrobe quite often it has more of a freak show feel to it because overall, she is really not all that attractive. Her face is nice enough. They have her in a terrible silver wig for the entire film and she has what I

Harry Reems is in fine form, porn star mustache ablazing. He probably liked the change of pace from his pornography career and he seems to delight in the scenes where he is killing people. Especially the strangulation murder of Eve.

Wishman is known for using no sound on set and usually shows the back of the head when people are talking or their feet. This one does a great deal of dubbing instead. Sure, there are some feet shots. It wouldn't be a Wishman flick without them.

Deadly Weapons is probably my least favorite of the two movies that Chesty did for Wishman. It is the darker of the two with more of a downbeat ending. I did think that her crawling to her father and gently laying her head on his chest like a good girl was kind of sweet.

Let's move on to the second feature in this article before we delve much deeper into the pair of films and how they work together.

DOUBLE AGENT 73

1974

Produced and Directed by Doris Wishman

Story by Judy Kushner

Starring Chesty Morgan, Frank Silvano, Saul Meth, Jill Harris, Louis Burdi, Peter Petrillo, Cooper Kent, Joseph Chiaro, Denise Purcell, Donny Lee, Kurt Brandt, Nat Perogine

Make Up by Miriam Meth

Edited by Louis Bundi

Director of Photography Yuri Haviv

The movie opens with a pair of guys playing cards. One has a huge birthmark on his face. While they are engrossed in the game someone is breaking into the house. He goes from room to room, rifling through drawers and closets until he finds a spool of microfilm in a small, ceramic jar. When he goes to leave the card players knock him out and drag him to the car. He gets free and runs off. They drive after him and run him down leaving him to die in the street.

Then we are off to a nudist colony and a rousing game of volleyball. Jane (Chesty Morgan) is sunning herself when she gets a call from the agency in New York. They need her back in the Big Apple for a mission. She needs to break up a huge heroin ring led by a mysterious man named Toplar. Toplar has never been photographed so they implant a XL-17 camera into her left breast so she can take pictures of the bad guys and get photographic evidence of Toplar. As she recovers the nurse (Denise Purcell) tries to slip her a knock out pill, but Jane is too smart for that. As the double agent reports back to her boss Jane strangles her with the phone cord. I did think it was funny that in both movies Denise Purcell met the same demise; death by strangulation. The deed done, Jane snaps a picture of the dead agent. I laughed every time she did this because she would move her breast up and then a loud camera shutter noise followed by a flash occurred. I have no idea where they hid the flash. Maybe the right breast. It is Chesty Morgan so there was room for an entire photography studio in there. For a secret boob camera the damned thing made quite a ruckus.

A coded message appears under the door giving her clues as to the whereabouts of her first bad guy at a loud, raucous club. The guy is the hood that was playing cards with Igor (Saul Meth) the man with the huge birthmark on his face. Jane finds him and they chat for a moment in front of a huge sheet of reflective material that is supposed to be the club.

Jane makes an excuse to slip away and goes to the club office. Using a mini bomb she blows the lock off the door and locates some evidence so, time to go topless and take some pictures. As she is doing that, the man from the club enters the room and rushes her. Jane knocks him down by smacking him with one of her boobs. She makes a run for it and gets to her car. The man follows close behind and the chase is on. It doesn't take long to catch up and soon Jane is in his car at his mercy. He drives her to a secluded place and tells her to get out. Always the Queen of Cool, Jane applies some lipstick before she bolts from the car. The hood smiles as he levels his pistol at her back. He doesn't notice Jane has left her lipstick behind.

The car explodes.

Igor calls a hitman (Kurt Brandt) to get rid of Jane. She is causing too much trouble.

Jane gets another coded message to meet her next contact at the zoo. Before she can leave her friend (Jill Harris) arrives for a visit. Jane goes out for a little bit while her friend decides to take a shower. The assassin arrives and takes out Jane's friend with a knife. Apparently Igor forgot to mention Jane's attributes because there is no way anyone would mistake this girl for Chesty Morgan. Jane comes back and discovers the body, but still needs to get to the zoo to meet her next contact. The man introduces himself as Atlantis 7 (Frank Silvano) and tells Jane that the boss sent him.

While they take a tour of the zoo, Igor calls the assassin and tells him he killed the wrong girl.

Jane, finished with her trip to the zoo heads home and gets herself a much deserved drink. The hitman arrives with a gun this time, but Jane is too smart for him. A ceramic pot on the bar issues out a stream of knock out gas and sends the hitman to the floor. Jane uses ice cubes to drown him to death and then its picture time!

She tries to get some rest when the phone rings. It is Tim a.k.a. Atlantis 7. He invites her out for a date and she agrees. The date ends up back at his place and they start making out.

I assume the date went well and it's the next day as Jane is rifling through someone's things in a room we haven't seen before. She is interrupted by a guy with a gun, but in one fluid movement she takes off one of her earrings and impales him in the throat with it from across the room. Another dead bad guy means more pictures!

Tim calls into to the boss to tell him that Jane is missing. The chief says she could be at the big horse race at the track and to go there to find her. Tim, who thinks he is falling for Jane goes to the race track to find her with no luck.

Jane is going through her list of people connected to the heroin ring and is waiting in the shower when a couple come home from the bar. He is drunk and she goes to freshen herself up. Jane knocks her out and ties her up. She rubs something on her breasts and goes into the bedroom where the man starts licking her breasts and dies. I assume it's some sort of poison. Pictures taken and the deed done Jane goes into the bathroom to wash off the poison.

Jane's next hit is Igor himself, but he gets the drop on her and ties her up. While he is beating her for information the woman Jane tied up earlier, Greta arrives and helps with the beating. Igor asks Great to go get food. While he is waiting he gets a call from Toplar. Jane uses a special ring to set off a charge that burns her bonds. Toplar has given instructions to release Jane so, when Great returns with the food Jane uses a broken bourbon bottle to kill them both. She takes the required pictures and is off.

Back at headquarters Tim tells the chief that he can't find Jane. The chief is in a panic because unbeknownst to anyone they had a bomb planted with camera and it is set to go off at any minute. Jane, beaten and exhausted staggers into the office. They manage to get the bomb out and the film developed. They check all of Jane's victims for the scar they need to identify Toplar. Unfortunately, during her make out session with Tim the camera went off and reveals a cross shaped scar on his ear lobe. Tim is actually Toplar!

The chief offers to handle the situation, but Jane says she will take care of it. She goes to Tim and confronts him. He admits to doing shady things, but now he loves her and wants to go straight and marry her. Jane's response is to pull out her gun and shoot him dead.

Tired from her ordeal she goes home and is greeted by a phone call from the Chief. He needs her for an assignment in Istanbul. She tells him no, but the film ends with a plane taking off so we know that she was a good agent and went to Istanbul.

Double Agent 73 is the better of the two Wishman/Chesty movies. As secret agent Jane she is ruthless. Her deadpan acting skills actually work better here than in *Deadly Weapons*. It gives her the look of a stone cold killer and the way she attacks without any thought makes her come across as a seasoned field agent. She is there to do a job. The odd part is that at no time does anyone mention heroin. Is it really the best way to stop a heroin ring by slaughtering everyone involved? I suppose it would work. And the agency is never identified so we have no idea if they are government sanctioned or some kind of shadow organization. The obvious answer is that it's an exploitation film showing off Chesty Morgan's obvious assets. I realize that the title is a play on words concerning those assets, but it does muddle things in that Chesty's character is not a double agent of any kind.

This was an extremely enjoyable film and I'm a little sad that it's the only one. Just for the storyline alone I would have watched continuing adventures of Chesty Morgan as a secret agent. I was also surprised that her accent is so thick that they had to dub her voice. The accent might have added some mystique to the character.

I did find it interesting that in both films the bad guys had a crossed shaped scar and were men close to the main character. I did find it odd that she didn't notice Tim's scar on his ear lobe before the big reveal at the end. His hair wasn't that long to cover it. In Deadly Weapons she had no idea that the scar was significant because she didn't know her father's double life as a gangster.

So, there you have the entire film career of Ms. Chesty Morgan. Exploitation film making in its purest form.

If your curiosity is piqued I suggest going to the web page The Rialto Report. There is a really recent interview with Chesty that is a fascinating read.

TURNING BACK THE HANDS OF SLIME

Back in the mid '70s, newspapers like The New York Daily News, The New York Post, and others carried ads for Triple X porn films. In the mid '80s, due to political pressure, these same papers refused to run these ads. Here's a sampling of some of the ads as well as flyers used to advertise films at the Fine Arts Theater of Adult Entertainment in Worcester, Mass.

DESIRE FOR MEN

Long Jeanne Silver gained notoriety with the 1977 production of *Long Jeanne Silver*. That title alone guaranteed her hall of fame status. Yet that film tends to overshadow her other work in the XXX field. Appearing in less than twenty features, Jeanne's work is long overdue for reappraisal. In this issue we'll take a look at her 1981 feature *Desire for Men*.

Written and directed by Carol Connors (who also stars) *Desire for Men* was filmed under the watchful eyes of the Mitchell Brothers. Connors is Jeanne, a "bonerfide" slut who lives with her mom (Laura Shawn). Herschel Savage is Paul…newly betrothed to Sue (Long Jeanne Silver). No sooner are they congratulated by Jeanne before she whisks Paul off to his new car in order to screw his brains out!

Jeanne continues to have her way with men…when she's not masturbating or doing exercises in her panties! She also finds time to take a shower wearing panties…strange. Anyhow Sue and Paul swing by Jeanne's house for some wine and food. Sue takes one too many swigs of booze and promptly passes out. Jeanne takes advantage of this, urging Paul to eat her pussy! She also instructs him to take advantage of his wife while she's out which he promptly does.

In order to deflect the sexual urges of Jeanne, Paul sets her up with his new boss Jacob (Lew Mann). They hit it off upon visiting a live sex act (where everyone is encouraged to participate). Incidentally this scene features some major players such as Erica Boyer and Nicole Black. Even though Sue appears to be in love with Jacob (even telling her mom that he's in line to become her husband) she still can't resist fucking other dudes. When a T.V. repairman (remember them?) shows up to fix Jeanne's boob tube it's Jeanne's pussy that gets fucked! Apparently her mom was upset that she missed the Barbara Walters special with Clint Eastwood and Charles Bronson!

The last sequence of the film is a nightmare where Jeanne takes on the role of a dominatrix. She whips and berates all of the people in her life including Sue. Sue in turn takes out her stump and proceeds to fuck Jeanne right in the pussy! Needless to say this entire sequence is nothing short of bizarre. It appears that she's worried about Jacob proposing to her so her inner demon comes out. Obviously I'm reading between the lines since the script is more sex than anything. Oddly enough the film abruptly ends when Jeanne catches her mom getting screwed by a black man (Darnell Mason)! What the fuck?!?!?

For about 60 minutes *Desire for Men* trots out typical XXX behavior before descending into foreign territory for the last 15. I have no idea what Connors was trying to prove with this story since things never get resolved. Her character is a slut; she screws a bunch of dudes and fears marriage…or something like that. Also one wonders how much 'directing' Connors really did since she's on screen for 80% of the film. Either way she does do a great job portraying a woman in heat, which incidentally disproves the theory that Connors was a 'dead fuck' on screen.

Today her claim to fame is the fact that she pushed Thora Birch out into the world but that wouldn't happen for another year when *Desire for Men* was rolling for the camera. Much like Long Jeanne Silver, Connors doesn't have a long list of credits but she was always memorable whenever she appeared on screen. As for her sexual prowess she didn't seem to be as daring as some of her co-stars. In fact during the nightmare scene it's Serena who gets penetrated by Long Jeanne Silvers stump (the end credits clearly point this out). However the scene is edited to at least give the view the illusion it's Connors who is getting serviced. Aside from that the editing is pretty choppy in other spots wondering who was falling asleep when they should have been doing their job!

Long Jeanne Silver will be making a rare appearance at the April 2015 Cinema Wasteland convention. One can only imagine what stories she will share with her adoring audience. Even with her limited screen time in *Desire for Men* it's obvious she had a knack for leaving an indelible mark on the viewer. Fans looking for quality smut circa 1981 need look no further! Track it down and see for yourself…

Made in the USA
Middletown, DE
01 February 2018